Greek Mythology

A Deeper Guide into the Amazing Myths and Legends of Greek Gods, Heroes, and Monsters

Joshua Brown

© **Copyright 2022 - All rights reserved.**

The content contained within this book may not be reproduced, duplicated or transmitted without direct written permission from the author or the publisher.

Under no circumstances will any blame or legal responsibility be held against the publisher, or author, for any damages, reparation, or monetary loss due to the information contained within this book. Either directly or indirectly.

Legal Notice:

This book is copyright protected. This book is only for personal use. You cannot amend, distribute, sell, use, quote or paraphrase any part, or the content within this book, without the consent of the author or publisher.

Disclaimer Notice:

Please note the information contained within this document is for educational and entertainment purposes only. All effort has been executed to present accurate, up to date, and reliable, complete information. No warranties of any kind are declared or implied. Readers acknowledge that the author is not engaging in the rendering of legal, financial, medical or professional advice. The content within this book has been derived from various sources. Please consult a licensed professional before attempting any techniques outlined in this book.

By reading this document, the reader agrees that under no circumstances is the author responsible for any losses, direct or indirect, which are incurred as a result of the use of information contained within this document, including, but not limited to, — errors, omissions, or inaccuracies.

Table of Contents

Introduction

Chapter 1: The Greek World

   The Heroic Age
   The Classical Period
   The Hellenistic Age

Chapter 2: In the Beginning

   The Creation of the World
   The Titans and the Olympians
   Pandora's Box
   Atlas and Prometheus

Chapter 3: Greek Gods and Goddesses

   The Gods of Mount Olympus
      Zeus
      Apollo
      Poseidon
      Hera
      Athena
      Aphrodite
      Ares
      Hephaestus
      Hades
      Demeter
      Dionysus
      Hermes
      Artemis
      Hestia
   Hera's Jealousy

    Hephaestus and Aphrodite
    Nymphs and Other Creatures

Chapter 4: The Children of the Gods

    The Children of Zeus
    Gods and Demigods
    The Birth of Heracles
    The Amazons

Chapter 5: Theseus and Other Heroes

    The Adventures of Theseus
    The Adventures of Perseus
    Jason and the Argonauts

Chapter 6: Tales of Zeus

    Zeus and Ganymede
    Zeus and Leda
    Zeus and Leto

Chapter 7: Tales of Apollo

    The Children of Apollo
    Apollo and Cassandra
    The Oracle of Delphi
    Laocoon
    Apollo and Hyacinthus

Chapter 8: The Twelve Labors of Heracles

    First Labor: The Nemean Lion
    Second Labor: The Hydra of Lernea
    Third Labor: The Wild Boar of Erymanthus
    Fourth Labor: The Hind of Ceryneia
    Fifth Labor: The Stymphalian Birds
    Sixth Labor: The Augean Stables
    Seventh Labor: The Cretan Bull

    Eighth Labor: The Horses of Diomedes
    Ninth Labor: The Girdle of the Amazon
    Tenth Labor: Geryon's Cattle
    Eleventh Labor: The Theft of Cerberus
    Twelfth Labor: The Apples of the Hesperides

Chapter 9: Lighter Tales of Greek Gods and Heroes

    Oedipus and his Children
    Artemis and Actaeon
    The Myth of Arachne
    Cupid and Psyche

Chapter 10: The Trojan War

    The Judgment of Paris
    Iphigenia in Aulis
    Achilles and Patroclus
    The Death of Achilles
    The Aftermath: Agamemnon and Clytemnestra

Chapter 11: Twenty Essential Facts about Greek Myth and Legend

    Fact One: Hades was not counted among the Olympians.
    Fact Two: The oldest texts that detail the Ancient Greek gods are the Iliad and the Odyssey.
    Fact Three: Hades was not only the name of the god of the underworld but also of the underworld itself.
    Fact Four: Before the Olympian gods, there were the Titans.
    Fact Five: The Olympian gods overthrew the Titans to become rulers of the universe.
    Fact Six: Zeus and his brothers drew lots to see who would control which of the three realms of the universe.

Fact Seven: Hera was not the first wife of Zeus.

Fact Eight: The exhaustive list of the Olympians is up for debate as some count Hestia among the number while others count Dionysus.

Fact Nine: The Romans drew most of their gods from the pantheon of Greek gods and goddesses.

Fact Ten: Most Greek cities had their main temple devoted to their patron god, but there would have been other temples devoted to the rest of the divinities, too.

Fact Eleven: Zeus won a bet when Tiresias deemed that he was right about sex and not Hera. (The goddess struck him blind as a punishment).

Fact Twelve: Hestia was the first of the Olympian gods to be born.

Fact Thirteen: Today, Cupid or Eros is often depicted as an infant, but he was originally described as a handsome youth.

Fact Fourteen: Both Apollo and Helios were technically gods of the sun.

Fact Fifteen: Both Artemis and Selene were goddesses of the moon.

Fact Sixteen: Zeus was known to take on disguises when courting his love interests.

Fact Seventeen: The Oracle at Delphi would give her prophecies in the form of cryptic answers to questions.

Fact Eighteen: One might say that it was Eris who was responsible for the Trojan War, not Paris.

Fact Nineteen: Greek mythology was practiced in regions outside the borders of modern-day Greece.

Fact Twenty: Much of our information on Greek mythology comes not from the Greeks, but the Romans.

List of Greek Gods and Other Characters

Frequently Asked Questions

Conclusion

Introduction

Greek Mythology is one of the great mythologies of the world. Tales of Greek gods and heroes have inspired countless generations in the Western world, and this trend shows no signs of letting up. These myths even inspired the Ancient Greeks to be better than they often were, even though the gods did not always set the best example. Today, Greek Mythology is taught in schools as part of an introduction to the West. Why? There are a number of reasons, but the struggle against the whims of life and the apparent fickleness of the gods so embodied the Greek experience as to make their mythology almost a representation of the human experience. In Greek mythology lay the foundations of Western art, literature, and philosophy.

Of course, to the Greeks, their mythology was merely the way the world was. The gods could be fickle and unkind and so too could life. Daily experiences were frequently rife with calamities that seemed to run contrary to reason, and this was also true for the heroes and mythological characters who would have their stories told in drama. To us, Oedipus may seem like a strange unfathomable character, but to the Greeks, he was man himself, burdened by the woes that characterized the life of men on Earth.

This chasm between ancient life and today is part of what makes mythology so interesting to study. When you take the time to learn about the gods and goddesses of a foreign people, you learn not only about who the people were and why they were, but you may even get a little glimpse at who you are. The drama of your life unfolds in ways that would have been understandable to people of the past even if they are occasionally not understandable to you.

In *Greek Mythology: A deeper guide into the amazing Myths and Legends of Greek Gods, Heroes, and Monsters* you will be introduced to the formative tales and characters of Greek myth. This introduction will allow you to understand how a people who lived more than two thousand years ago understood and experienced the world. These people may have been different from you, but it can be argued that the basics of life have not changed much in two thousand years (if at all). Human beings still experience the same loves, rages, and disappointments much as they did back then. These types of emotions were well encapsulated in Greek legend, which often takes the form of an elaborate drama.

To be honest, the drama is the best way to describe Greek myth and legend. Perhaps this is why the Greeks were the inventors of drama as we understand it today. The relationships between the gods, and between gods and mortals often had an emotional character that is seldom found in other mythologies. The Greek gods were jealous and vengeful. They loved and hated. They projected their frustrations onto others. In *Greek Mythology*: *A deeper guide into the amazing Myths and Legends of Greek Gods, Heroes, and Monsters*, you will learn of the loves of Zeus and of Apollo, and of the jealousies of Hera and Mars. These gods played out their emotions in a highly human fashion.

But some of the most interesting characters are actually the human ones. Few tales are as amazing as that of Theseus and the Minotaur. There was also the love of Theseus for Ariadne and Phaedra. Of course, there was Perseus and Andromeda, and Andromeda's mother Cassiopeia who was placed among the stars. The Greeks were very familiar with the tale of how Perseus slew the gorgon, Medusa. These were stories that children of the time were well-versed in just as children of today can recount the exploits of their favorite cartoon characters.

Naturally, Heracles was a character that the Greeks often wrote about. His exploits were dramatized in the theaters of their cities and large towns. His labors were reenacted at religious festivals as sort of a reminder that life was hardest of all for the great. The twelve labors of Heracles, indeed, seemed to be another representation of life itself, embodying the reality that life was a constant struggle and one that was sometimes lost. Perhaps all mythologies had this underlying message.

Everyone reading *Greek Mythology: A deeper guide into the amazing Myths and Legends of Greek Gods, Heroes, and Monsters* to learn about Greek myths and legends has their own reason for doing so. Some read because they hope to better understand how people of the past thought, perceived and lived. Reading about Greek myth allows one to understand in this fashion because the exploration of myth is practically a journey into the mind of another. When one thinks of the great compendium that is mythology and all of the men whose words and ways of storytelling contributed to this myth and legend, it really seems to be the mind of many others. Mythologies are created by men, by people, and they give a strong indication of the manner in which such people perceive the world.

What one learns from Greek myth is that the Ancient Greeks saw the world as filled with good things as well as bad. They saw man as engaged in constant struggle with himself. Man loved too much and this love often roped him into trouble, trouble that was not easily escaped from (just ask Zeus). Man struggled against fate and in so doing caused that fate to become a reality. It seemed that Man was destined to always be fooled in his attempts at peace, and many Greek myths (if not most) seem to end unhappily. But then we read about Odysseus and how he managed to return home to his wife Penelope, showing that loyalty - the loyalty the twain had for each other - was rewarded by the gods.

This is what Greek Mythology is, more so than other mythologies. It is a compendium of lessons that teach men how to deal with the harsh occurrences of the world. Remember that the Greeks did not live in fertile land. They created their civilization on stones and mountainsides. They created cities out of the rubble, polices that hugged the seas and waterways that abutted the Mediterranean. The Greeks were subject to the whims of weather and the anger of the sea. They had to learn to deal with and understand a world that was often cruel or perish if they did not.

But the Greeks did not perish. They turned their faces up to gods that were like themselves. They learned to navigate a world that was frequently inhospitable and hostile towards them. They fought the Persians at Thermopylae and Marathon and won. They even fought each other: sometimes winning, sometimes losing. These are the people whose belief system and manner of living are encapsulated in the myths and legends that are left to us today.

In Greek Mythology, you will learn who these ancient people were. You will learn to empathize with them, even though they have been dead for thousands of years. This will entail loving the way that they loved, and feeling rage just how they might feel rage. You will understand the disappointments of Oedipus, Atlas, and Prometheus because you feel them too. You will identify with Hera's rage about Io, and feel the surprise that Zeus felt when Athena burst fully-formed from his head. This is what it means to immerse yourself in Greek myth.

This emersion is something the Romans understood well. Roman myth really is Greek myth, even if the Romans kept idols of their original gods locked deep in their cupboards. The Romans took most of the Greek myth and made it into their own over a period of hundreds of years.

Indeed, the Romans adopted Greekness so early in their history that it is nearly impossible to know precisely when this process began. Greek gods received Roman names. Zeus became Jupiter and Hera Juno. Ares became Mars and Aphrodite Venus. The Romans even worked Greek myth into their own history, describing themselves as being descended from Aeneas after he left Troy.

This history is important to understand because it is lurking in the myths and legends that have been passed down to us. Although we do not always see the hand of the historian when we read the mythological tale, the hand is there. A skillful historian will understand how the story may have changed over time. They may perceive that Aphrodite did not originate with the Greeks but began as Astarte and Ishtar in the Near East. They realize that Dionysus came laughing and singing from the hills north of Greece. The historian can see how two legendary characters or gods became one as civilization progressed.

For this reason, we begin our survey of Greek myth and legend by exploring the world of the Greeks. To understand them, it becomes necessary to learn what formed them: to learn the land where some ancestors sprung autochthonous and where others conquered and enslaved.

Indeed, the history of the Greeks is rife with the legacy of this conquest, particularly when one examines the Spartans who basically lived as conquerors in a land they had earned by force. This brief exploration of the Greek world will be undertaken in the first chapter.

Like all mythologies, Greek Mythology has its foundation myths. These are the formative stories about the gods, giants, and monsters that existed at the time of the beginning of the world. Some will be familiar with the story of Pandora's box. Others may have heard the stories of Prometheus and Atlas. These stories more than any other give a sense of the manner in which the Greeks perceived their world so we will begin here. This survey will be undertaken in the second chapter.

At the center of every system of myths and legends are the gods themselves. Some religions believe that Man has been created in God's image while others believe that the gods created man because they were bored. Whatever line the particular religion takes, a review of the gods will give a sense of the gestalt of the religion: the tempo of the belief system. The drumbeat of Greek belief is one that beats quickly like a heartbeat. It is the sound of a life that has been lived in the present. The gods of Greek myth are very much creatures of the present and their story will be told in the third chapter.

It is the story of the many loves of Zeus. It is the story of the great jealousy of Hera. There are many other tales besides. As in some other mythologies, the main group of Greek gods had to overthrow the gods who came before them. This was the war between the Olympians and the infamous Titans. In Greek Mythology, the goal is for the reader to understand who the Greeks were by learning what they believed. A portion of this entails understanding which gods they revered and which they feared. Gods of war were not as important to the Greeks as they were to Norsemen. An understanding of this dimension on the subject will also be examined in the third chapter.

In many mythologies, the children of the gods occupy a special, luminal place. They are often neither gods nor mortals. In Greek myth, they have usually termed demigods, a tacit acknowledgment that they were more than mere mortal man. In the fourth chapter, we will explore the place that these children of the gods occupied, and how their place in the Ancient Greek religion was not quite the same as it was in other religious belief systems.

Heroes occupy a critical place in every mythology. Heroes more than any other represent the role of the listener. Most mythological tales were stories told not unlike gossip, only the storytellers were often men who plied a craft rather than merely told tall tales.

There was a point to the story, and when you examine the stories of the heroes you learn what that point is. The stories of heroes were meant to teach life lessons, and it is in hearing the stories of Theseus, Perseus, Achilles, and others that we learn the sorts of lessons the Greeks thought it important to teach.

As the king of the Olympian gods, Zeus presided over the Greek pantheon. He was also the sky God and father of other gods, such as Apollo, Athena, Hermes, and Artemis. Zeus was the center of many tales as he was often the invisible hand spurring a hero towards this or that. But Zeus occasionally played the role of the protagonist. In the sixth chapter, we will learn tales of Zeus, most of which revolve around the many loves he nurtured with mortals.

Apollo was another Greek god who served as an important fixture of myth. Indeed, the worship of Apollo was so important that he had his own oracle, the Oracle of Delphi, who was regarded as the most important in the Greek world. Apollo, god of the sun, was also otherworldly handsome so many of his own tales, too, revolve around love.
Many of them do, but not all as Apollo was associated with moderation. In Apollo, the Greeks encapsulated many of their ideals on manhood, much as the Norse did with Thor.

Apollo's tales will be explored in *Greek Mythology: A deeper guide into the amazing Myths and Legends of Greek Gods, Heroes, and Monsters* to develop a picture of this god and what he meant to those who worshipped him.

Heracles is one of the most important characters of Greek myth and legend. He embodied brute strength, though, like Apollo, he also represented maleness. Some of the great sculptures of the Greek period depicted a muscled, powerful Heracles, a demigod whom the Romans knew as Hercules. Though the Roman name is the more famous, this demigod's land was Greece and nearly all the tales of his life take place in Greek lands. In chapter eight, we will examine the twelve labors of Heracles and the statement that they made about the struggles of man.

There are many other characters whose tales need to be examined to get the full picture of Greek myth and legend. Among these is Oedipus, a name that has become famous because of Greek tragedy. In the ninth chapter, we will examine tales of some of the other characters in Greek myth. Though not all should be termed light, these lighter tales often focus on Man and his hubris against the gods rather than on the spillover of godly conflict into the realm of Man.

No story embodies this spillover from the gods than the story of the Trojan War.

Told in the Iliad, the first long work of fiction in Europe, this story sums up the story of the Greeks in a way that few stories can summarize a people. It is a story of how the Greeks fought the Trojans and even turned against one another, all for the love of a woman: the most beautiful woman in the world. She was Helen of Troy, wife of the King of Sparta, and she was taken by fair Paris to his home kingdom of Troy in what is now Turkey. In the tenth chapter, you will discover the most epic tale of heroes ever written.

Ancient Greece still exists around you. You see it in the government buildings that are fashioned to hearken back to Greece and Rome. You see it in the so-called Greek system in colleges and universities. And it is evident in many ways in popular culture, especially in film, literature, and television. Ancient Greece is as alive today as it was three thousand years ago. The important question to ask is why. By the time you finish reading Greek Mythology, you will have learned the answer to that question.

Chapter 1: The Greek World

The Ancient Greeks were very much a product of their environment. They were the beneficiaries of the fruits that the Mediterranean Sea had to offer it, plying this blessed waterway with their triremes. They colonized the coast of Asia Minor and Southern Italy, spreading their beliefs and way of life to distant shores. Their society enriched itself over time, becoming advanced in science and philosophy. But the Greeks never stopped looking to the gods for guidance for it was their religion which made them Greek. Socrates learned what could happen when one veered too far away from godly ways.

But, for the most part, the gods looked approvingly on the activities of their subjects. They approved of the colonization efforts; they certainly approved of the massive temples erected all over the Greek world. They probably even approved of the philosophical meanderings, as long as they did not question the paramount place of the gods. Indeed, Greek history seemed to be a lesson on how the gods were always right. When you challenged their authority, when you aimed too high, you risked bringing all crashing down.

In this first chapter, we will undertake a brief survey of Greek history, taking into account the Greek religion.

As the Greeks became exposed to foreign people, they certainly adopted new gods, new language about religion, and new ways of worship. Greek society was always somewhat on the move, and the gods had to find a way to work themselves into that dynamics. Here we will discuss briefly the main ages of Greek history: The Heroic Age, the Classical Period, and the Hellenistic Age.

The Heroic Age

There is still debate about who wrote the Iliad, one of the most famous, and certainly among the most important, works of world literature. Historians have ascribed this work to a man named Homer, but it has been proposed that this great work was written by several authors in about the 9th century BC. At the very least, this work was compiled around that time and it pertained to events that had taken place around three centuries before.

Of course, we can now say that at least part of the Trojan War - the subject of the Iliad - appears to be true, but that statement could not be made two short centuries ago. The work of Heinrich Schliemann, a German businessman, and archaeologist allowed history books to be rewritten. Troy was no longer a myth. It was a real city that existed on the coast of Asia Minor. Schliemann's finds reveal that Troy was the largest city in the region during its height, more than 3000 years ago. This would place the greatness of Troy - a city whose destruction was ordained by the gods - at a few hundred years before Homer is believed to have lived.

This was the Heroic or Archaic Age of Greece. This is Greece before the explosion of artistic culture that has been left to us in the form of exquisitely decorated bowls, sculpture, and architecture. This is Greece before the philosophies of Plato and Socrates, the histories of Thucydides and Xenophon, and the plays of Aeschylus. This was Greece in a time when the gods were still very much real. They came down from the heights of Mount Olympus to interfere in the lives of men. They directed events for their own pleasure and often to the detriment of Man.

Troy technically was a non-Greek culture, but enough remains in the Greek world to attest to what the Greeks themselves built.

The remains of the Argolid and Crete give evidence of a vibrant culture where the men and women lived in sizeable towns. They were ruled by kings and left elaborate graves. This was different from the Greece of the Classical period. Classical Greeks primarily lived in oligarchies, although there were some notable democracies in Athens and other places. The Heroic Age of Homer was the period that later Greeks looked to as the age of their heroes. To them, Achilles, Theseus, Heracles, and others were men who actually lived, and they lived during this time.

What is important to the student of myths and legends to know is that the Greeks left few written records from this time. There were likely several reasons for this. This was a time not only of war but of cultural solidification. Greek society was in the process of being formed into a shape that would be recognizable to us today. The Greeks were actually composed of several different groups who were collectively known as Hellenes or Greeks. Some of these groups were descended from the earliest inhabitants of the land while others were descended from invaders.

The Greeks of the Classical period saw themselves as being composed of three major divisions: the Dorians, Ionians, and Aeolians. Each group spoke a dialect of Greek and had traditions that marked them out as a Dorian or Ionian.

For example, Dorian societies divided their group into a certain number of tribes while Ionians had a different number. The Spartans were Dorians while the Athenians were Ionians. This meant that the Spartans were descended from relatively recent invaders while the Athenians were descended from settlers of a much earlier period. These divisions were very real.

For example, male gods tended to be more popular among Dorians like the Spartans and Corinthians, while older groups revered female gods or gods of very ancient origin. This dichotomy between a male-centered pantheon and gynocentric worship is somewhat subliminal, but it is there. It is apparent to those paying attention that there were several important female divinities in the Greek pantheon, forming a contrast to other mythologies where there may be one or two. The Greeks had Athena, Hera, Artemis, Aphrodite, and others, suggesting a pantheon where some gods were more ancient than others.

There were practical differences in the various groups in Greece, too. Besides some differences in language, Greeks might form alliances based on the historical group to which they belonged.

So Ionian Greeks might team up against Dorians like the Spartans, or they might share religious festivals in common. They might even claim a mythological person as their ancestors, such as Heracles or Achilles.

The legacy of invasion in the Heroic Age persisted into the Classical and Hellenistic periods. The Spartans were conscious that they were invaders who had subjugated the Messenians and Arcadians who had come before them, turning them into helots and slaves. One day, these subjugated people would overthrow their Dorian conquerors, turning Sparta from a Greek power into a week, depopulated backwater.

The Classical Period

The Classical Period represents the height of Greek civilization. It was a golden age of art, literature, and practically all forms of cultural life. During this time, the Greeks bested their enemies and spread their influence to most regions of the Mediterranean. The Mediterranean Sea might have become a Greek lake and not a Roman one if it was not for the propensity of the Greeks to war amongst each other. Where the Romans were good at assimilating their enemies, the Greeks were good at... well, remaining divided until this division eventually destroyed them.

One of the most important events to occur during the Heroic or Archaic Age was the colonization of much of the Mediterranean. This colonization was very significant because it resulted in Greek culture and Greek gods being adopted by the Romans. The Roman pantheon of gods is essentially Greek with the addition of some peripheral characters that never really developed a story. Roman culture, therefore, has a strong undercurrent of the Greek culture that preceded it. Even Roman historiography continues the work of the Greek historians who came first.

The Classical Period on the surface appears to see a gradual diminishing of the influence of the gods, but the reality is much more complex. The Greeks actually lived in fear of their divinities. Though Greek drama appears to suggest that the gods were both fickle and very human, the Greeks knew better than to anger them. Angering the gods would be enough to bring a city-state or people crashing down, a fate they were wise enough to try and avoid.

Indeed, the gods almost took on a political connotation. The glory of Athens contributed to the glory of Athena. The Athenians erected monuments to their gods and heroes, like the Parthenon, Eretheum, and the so-called Theseum.

This happened all over the Greek world. The Argives built monuments to Hera and the Ephesians built monuments to Artemis. In a way, the Classical period saw an increase in monuments to the gods even as society became in some ways more secular. It was almost a sort of Counter-Reformation that occurred minutely across all the city-states.

Of course, many of these cities built such monuments after the Persian War, when cities were vying for influence in the newly freed Greek world. This is certainly what Athens did. Athena became not only an important goddess in general but the symbol of the preeminence of Athenai, the city of Athena. Her wisdom was theirs. It seemed only natural that plays, art, and literature should flourish, even if there was a subversive or sacrilegious element. That element could always be purged, as happened around the time of Socrates when the Athenian Republic was at its lowest.

There, indeed, is another point to explore: a very important concept in Greek mythology. The Greek gods were gods of republics as well as kingdoms. They were the divinities of the Greek city-States as well as the kingdoms of Macedon and Epirus. Gods are by nature conservative, but the Greek gods seemed to be a little more free-thinking. It seemed the Greek gods, too, created Man in their own image. Come what may, the Greek gods would remain characteristically Greek.

What did that mean? The answer to that question would become more obvious as Greek civilization declined. Of course, it never completely disappeared as the Romans continued it, but politically the Greeks would never be the same once Alexander came onto the scene.

The defeat of the Persians in the 5th century left a power vacuum that had to be filled. Athens, as one of two preeminent Greek states during the Persians Wars (the other was Sparta), rose to fill the space by forming the Delian League out of Ionian states that were now free. It was called Delian because it was centered on the island of Delis. It became an Athenian Empire in all but name, and the rivalry between Athens and Sparta eventually boiled over into a war, the Peloponnesian War, which would last for nearly 30 years.

This was spilled over into the Greek colonies of Magna Grecia, foreshadowing the eclipse of Greece proper by the fertile colonies to the West like Syracuse and Tarentum, cities which still exist to this day. As most of you already know, Athens was defeated in this war, which led to the formation of a conservative government.

A Spartan-led Greece was short-lived, as the Spartans really did not have the propaganda machine and mass appeal that Athens could muster.

Thebes rose briefly, but, in the end, the Greeks would be overrun by a tribal people to the North, the Macedonians, a huge event that would eventually spell the beginning of the end of the Greek gods.

The Hellenistic Age

The Greek gods never seemed to have a problem with war. Their concern seemed always to be that their altars were kept lit and their sacrifices were not forgotten. But it would be a too great propensity for war that would eventually lead the Greeks into problems. A Greece always at war was a perfect open door for a well-organized outsider to enter. In this case, it was Macedon, led by the one-eyed King Philip.

Philip of Macedon was the father of Alexander the Great. The world was too small for him so he wept when he realized there were no more worlds left to conquer. Alexander, out of all Greek historical figures, seems more like a legend than a real person. He was larger than life, but it would be he that would spell the beginning of the end for the Olympians.

What did Alexander do that was so wrong? Alexander realized that the Greeks and Macedonians would have to live with Persians, Egyptians, and others, and that meant that a little bit of cultural exchange would have to take place.

That meant more than intermarrying. It meant that the Greeks would have to get used to gods like Isis, Osiris, and others. Simple enough. There was always room for more gods up on Mount Olympus. The problem comes about when those gods are of a different character. The Eastern and African gods were the divinities of autocrats, not free men. Indeed, as Greek democracy died with the rise of Alexander, so too would the Greek gods themselves.

Chapter 2: In the Beginning

Every mythological tradition has stories of creation. These creation myths set the framework for how everything else is learned unfolds. So the listener hears the stories of the creation of the universe, of the Titans and Olympians, of Pandora's Box and Atlas, and they learn how to interpret everything that comes afterward. This is essentially the role of mythology in societies: to help ordinary people understand how to live in their world and relate to one another. So men and women learned that the gods should not be angered because they were prone to vengeance and that the gods also must be appeased in order to obtain what wanted from them.

Though Greek mythology is often thought of as the benchmark by which other mythologies are compared, there are some unique aspects to Greek myth and legend that set it apart. The Greek pantheon featured male and female gods, both of which were prominent in the web of Greek myth and legend. The Greeks placed emphasis on others such as demigods, nymphs and naiads, and heroes who seemed to occupy the middle ground between god and man.

The Creation of the World

The Ancient Greeks believed that life sprang from nothingness: the vast void of space. From this abyss, Gaia sprung into life. Gaia was the goddess of earth, the personification of the planet. Gaia gave birth to two children without having to mate. These sons were Uranus and Pontus. Gaia also gave birth to several children who were monsters as well. But the youngest of the godly sons of Gaia was Cronus, youngest of the Titans. Cronus was actually fathered by Uranus, who was therefore both the father and half-brother of Cronus.

Cronus's brothers had been imprisoned in Tartarus by Uranus because this god had been displeased with the offspring that Gaia had created. Cronus attacked his father, freeing the monster children of Gaia from their imprisonment in Tartarus. Cronus felt pride at his overthrow of his father and became the new king of the gods. Cronus also disliked his brother monsters and imprisoned them back in Tartarus, which caused the anger of his mother.

During this time, the first humans were born. They lived for thousands of years, maintaining a youthful look. During this time, the race of humans intermingled with the gods, living in relative peace together.

During this time also, Cronus married his sister Rhea and gave birth to several children including Demeter, Hades, Hestia, Hera, Poseidon, and Zeus. Cronus sported a scythe as a weapon, and he was associated with fertility and the harvest.

The Titans and the Olympians

Cronus began to despise his children because he feared that one day, they would overthrow him the way he had overthrown his father. Cronus solved the problem of the threat his children posed by eating them after each was born. But Rhea managed to save her youngest child. She gave her husband a stone wrapped in swaddling clothes instead of the child that had been born. This child was Zeus. Zeus was spirited away to Crete where he was raised in secrecy.

Zeus discovered a potion that would force Cronus to spit up the children that he had swallowed. Cronus no longer feared being overthrown as he believed all of his children were a god. Zeus came to Cronus disguised as a cupbearer. Zeus gave his father the potion, which caused Cronus to vomit. The stone was the first to come out, followed by Poseidon, Hades, Hera, Hestia, and the others. They were vomited up in the order reverse to how they had been followed.

Zeus feared that the Titans would come to the aid of Cronus. Cronus was weak because of the potion. Zeus went down to Tartarus where he freed his uncle gods. These included cyclopes. Zeus and his siblings went to Mount Olympus where they settled and plotted against Cronus. The cyclopes fashioned weapons for the gods, including the trident for Poseidon and the lightning bolt for Zeus. The Titans were defeated in battle, in part because of the powerful weapons they had. Because Atlas had led them, he was punished with having to hold the world on his back. This was a common image in Greek art in ancient times.

The Titans were locked in Tartarus and guarded by monsters. The universe was divided up among the gods. Poseidon was granted the seas and oceans while Hades was granted the underworld, filled with both defeated gods and humans. Zeus was the ruler of the world and overall king of the gods.

Pandora's Box

The first woman was called Pandora. It was said that she was breathed to life by the breath of the god of fire, Hephaestus. The Olympian gods granted her many gifts, including the gift of emotion, the ability to create objects with her hands which came with a fine attention to detail, and the gift of language.

From Zeus, Pandora received two additional gifts: a curious nature and a large box that was screwed shut tightly. But Pandora was told the contents of the box were not for human eyes. Was curiosity a blessing or a curse?

Pandora fell in love with Epimetheus, a Titan. Epimetheus was the brother of Prometheus, who himself would be punished for giving humans fire. Pandora was excited by what she found on earth. She was pleasant but fiery and impatient. Pandora could not resist the urge to open the box. She felt that the contents of the box were itching to be freed. She began to be obsessed with the box. She felt the box calling to her: "Pandora, Pandora." Pandora could not resist the urge to open it and she cracked the box just to get a peek inside. But the box flew open and all the monsters and evil things flew out. Zeus had used the box to trap those things that would bring evil into the world. Pandora began to weep at the evil she had unleashed into the world. Pandora opened the box again and saw a beam of light come out. This beam of light was hope and Pandora's heart was somewhat set at ease that she had released this into the world, too, to temper the effects of what she had done.

Atlas and Prometheus

As has already been stated, Atlas was the leader of the Titans in their war against the Olympians.

Atlas was the son of a certain Iapetus by Clymene. Atlas was alone among the Titans in not being confined to Tartarus, which seems to be where the ancient gods exiled all those who were defeated or whom they just did not like or wish to see much of. Atlas's punishment was to carry upon his shoulders the sky until the end of time.

Prometheus was another Titan, and possibly the full-brother to Atlas. Prometheus was said to be the son of Iapetus by a woman who may have been Clymene. He was the brother of the Epimetheus who married Pandora. Prometheus was notable in Greek myth for a number of reasons. Some said that he was the creator of man. Most famously (or perhaps, more accurately), Prometheus was the one to give fire to mankind. To add godly insult to injury, he also taught men how to use the fire he had given them. In addition, it has been said that Prometheus also taught men other arts, like ocean navigation, medicine, metalworking, writing, and architecture.

Zeus was angered that Prometheus had "stolen" fire and given it to mankind. For this, the king of the gods had to come up with a creative punishment. The punishment was to have Prometheus tied and bound to a mountain, where an eagle constantly picked at his liver all day long for eternity.

But Prometheus healed nightly, meaning that he could not die and be relieved of his pain, but must continually suffer it anew. It would be Heracles who would rescue Prometheus. But Zeus was not done with the Titan. To punish mankind for their covetousness, Zeus gave Pandora a box full of evil and sent her into the world, as we have already seen.

Chapter 3: Greek Gods and Goddesses

Greek mythology, more than any other mythical tradition, was really a drama of the gods. The gods and goddesses of the Greek world seemed to be people, just with greater power and influence than mortals. Their lives were filled with the same sort of petty dramas of mortals, and they were not above squabbling with one another in very human ways. But the gods were gods nonetheless, with control of the sky, elements, emotions, and everything else that fell within the purview of deities. The gods made sure that mortals never forgot who they were and why they were.

In this chapter, we will be introduced to the Greek gods and goddesses, who sat at the center of Greek myth.

Indeed, even stories that had a human lead, like the legends of Perseus, Theseus, Jason, Paris, and others: these myths seemed to be as much about the gods as the humans since there was always a god in the background motivating this or that or interfering with this or that. Understanding the belief system of the Ancient Greeks requires that you understand their gods. The Greek gods were not like the Norse gods. They seemed to be gods of pleasure more than gods of war, and they were fond of consorting with mortals and interfering in the fabric of their lives. Perhaps the message was that there was godliness in all men, or, at the very least, that there was a certain humanity to the gods.

The Gods of Mount Olympus

The Greek gods and goddesses resided upon Mount Olympus. Mount Olympus was a real place. It was located in Thessaly, in Northern Greece, and it must have seemed to the Greeks a likely place for the gods to live. Greece was a place where there were mountains and high places than there were arable ones, and it was only natural that they would place their god at the highest place in this part of the world. This white top mountain looms over Greece, a place filled with mountains, and it was to Mount Olympus that the ubiquitous shepherd and fisherman of Greece looked.

Of course, Greece was also a land of sea and seafarers, but the gods responsible for those affairs lived on Mount Olympus, too. The Olympian gods were not the first gods, as we have already seen. The Olympians replaced the Titans, the gigantic gods who preceded them. It is interesting that many mythologies place giants before even the gods. The Norse did the same with their Jotunn, the giants who were fed by the cow of the universe Audhumla even before the sons of Borr; that is, Odin and his brothers.

It almost seems as if early Man remembered a distant past when everything was gigantic. Indeed, Greek mythology becomes about Man overcoming his environment in the same way as other mythologies do. In Norse mythology, the gods and other creatures seem to be earthly manifestations of this or that rather than characters with distinct identities. Although this is not entirely the case with Greek myth and legend, there is some of that color to the Greek stories, too. We will begin our survey of the gods and goddesses and their place in Greek myth by being introduced to them individually. These gods were Zeus, Apollo, Poseidon, Hera, Athena, Aphrodite, Ares, Hephaestus, Hades, Demeter, Dionysus, Hermes, and Artemis. They each had stories of their own, and each played a role in the general fabric of Greek life.

Zeus

Most mythological traditions had a father figure, a king of sorts who presided over the other gods as a father-king presides over his kid, and this was the role that Zeus filled among the Olympian gods. Zeus was not only the king of the gods, but he was the father of several of them. Zeus features in many myths of the Greeks, even if he is on the sidelines interfering in one way or the other. The role that Zeus played perhaps echoes the central emphasis that patriarchal societies placed on the patriarch: the head of both nuclear family and clan.

But Zeus was not alone in heading his clan, and this is something that Greek writers never let us forget. Zeus presided over the Olympians with Hera by his side. Indeed, Zeus sometimes seems to play the role of fixer to Hera's instigator. Hera is angered by this or that, and Zeus has to fix it. Zeus has done this or that to infuriate Hera and now he has to find a way to placate her. The relationship between these two gods seemed to echo the travails of marriage, but in the end, they always remain together. No matter how often Zeus's eye may wander, it is always to Hera that he returns. The essential patriarchy of both Greece and Rome is therefore mitigated by the ever-present woman-figure that will be explained in more detail later.

As nearly all civilizations known to us were patriarchal, there are echoes of Zeus - or what we might term Zeus-like figures - across most mythologies. Odin might be said to be a Zeus-like figure in Norse myth. Odin was also a god of the sky and weather, and he presided over the Norse equivalent of Mount Olympus: Asgard. The Norse were obsessed with war and halls that seemed to glorify war or serve a purpose in war, so Odin presided over Valhalla, which had thousands of halls were warriors might march through after they were honored for valor in death.

Zeus did not have the same explicitly warlike function in Greek myth that other, similar figures had in their own mythological belief systems. That being said, as king of the gods it was necessary to honor Zeus if one hoped to be victorious in war, or simply successful in this endeavor or that. As king of the gods he presided over all things and it was necessary that he be honored. As the sort of alpha male of Mount Olympus, Zeus fathered numerous children, including the gods Apollo, Artemis, Hermes, and Dionysus. In Roman myth, Zeus was known as Jupiter, and he served the same function for them that he did for the Greeks.

Apollo

Apollo was arguably the second most important god in Greek mythology. As god of the son, he was responsible for the light that provided men with heat in the daytime and sunshine when it was time to sow. Apollo was also associated with handsomeness among men and masculinity in general. Apollo is sort of a strange god as he seems to be sort of a mesh of a Greek element and a non-Greek element. Indeed, Apollo was the god the Greeks believed to be the advocate or embodiment of moderation, and it seemed that the god himself embodied a moderation between two disparate elements.

One element of Apollo seemed to be a sort of Near Eastern sun god.

This sort of god would likely have been appeased with ample sacrifices, and in some places was probably more important that Zeus, or whatever the local variant of Zeus was. It is important to explore this idea as Greek mythology does seem to represent an amalgamation of local belief systems. So, Apollo really represented the cynicism of different gods, creating a god who was both sun god and something else. Though we may say that there was something non-Greek about Apollo, the aesthetic element at least appears particularly Greek. Greek society was just as patriarchal as Rome, if not more, and an emphasis on male beauty and power as two sides of the same coin seems to be a natural extension of this androcentrism.

As we have already seen, there were Apollo-like figures in other belief systems. Although other mythologies do not always have a male sun god, a god with an association with nature or an element of nature that is also associated with maleness and masculinity is not uncommon. It is hard to say who the equivalent of Apollo would be in Norse belief; perhaps it would be Thor or Baldr. Apollo was one of the few Greek gods who kept his name in Roman myth, although he had to compete with other gods that had a similar function, like Sol, Mithras, Elagabalus, and others. As Helios, Apollo was the embodiment of the sun; in this guise, he was sometimes known as Apollo Helios. There were many places sacred to him, including the island of Delos, the island of Rhodes, Delphi, and others. There would have been temples or sacred places to Apollo in most Greek cities.

Poseidon

This is a useful place to mention the idea of a city being devoted to a god, or under the patronage of a god. So in Greek mythology and belief, we can talk about this or that city being sacred to this or that god. This meant that the people of that place would have regarded a particular god as their patron deity, even though they would have worshipped other gods as well.

This might also mean that people from other cities might come to a particular shrine in order to honor the god of that city. This was the case of the Temple of Artemis at Ephesus or the shrine of Aesculapius at Epidaurus.

Now onto Poseidon. Poseidon was the god of the sea. Most people that lived in places bordering the sea had a sea god, and as the Greeks were primarily a seafaring people it stands to reason that they would not only have a Poseidon but that Poseidon would be important. Poseidon was the protector of the creatures of the sea as well as men who traveled on the sea. So he would have been prayed to by fishermen and sailors going off to war alike.

As king of the sea, Poseidon had some accoutrements that made him rather interesting among the gods. His weapon was the three-pronged staff known as the triton. He was often depicted with this symbol in sculpture and painting alike. He was also often depicted with a crown and one that might have elements of the sea like seashells or conchs. Poseidon presided over the humanoid creatures of the sea and of water, like nymphs and nereids. Where the Norse had their obsession with fantastic creatures like elves, dwarfs, and the like, the Greeks were obsessed with the personifications of bodies of water. This sea-fixation is a characteristically Greek "thing" and it is important to take note of it here. Poseidon was worshipped in many Greek cities, and he had a famous temple at Marathon near Athens and at Paestum in Southern Italy.

Hera

Hera occupied an important place in Mount Olympus. Her title was queen, as the wife of Zeus, the king, but she was more than this. Hera had a role that was nearly as important as that of her husband. She was associated with the role of wife, domestic life, and motherhood. She would have been prayed to before marriage or before birth.

Because she was associated with wives and motherhood, she seemed also to be important in creation:

creating a trifecta of female gods who had a generative role, namely Athena (as the generator of wisdom), Aphrodite (as generator of love), and Hera (as a generator of domesticity).

In spite of Hera's association with the family, wives, children, and other domestic arts, her own domestic life was somewhat of a mess. She was constantly in a state of outrage over the frequent infidelities of her husband. Zeus fathered children with goddesses, nymph, and human alike. He really did not discriminate when it came to love, and so too did Hera not discriminate when it came to the targets of her rage. Greek myth is rife with the anger of Hera, and this dynamic seemed to serve a role in the Greek psyche as some sort of reflection of the realities of life. Hera was worshipped in many places, but Argos was the city most sacred to her. In Roman myth, she was known as Juno, the wife of Jupiter.

Athena

Athena was one of the most important Greek divinities: a goddess associated with wisdom. This goddess was also associated with war, and she is generally shown if not dressed in armor at least wearing a helmet and carrying a spear. One wonders how significant Athena would be if it were not for Athens. It is an interesting idea to explore, as the individual Greek gods were almost like the sports teams of the ancient worlds. Athena was to Athens what the Penguins are to Pittsburgh, or the Celtics are to Boston. Athens played an important role in the propaganda regarding Athena, and she, in turn, protected the city that had been named after her.

Athena is interesting for other reasons as well. Greek legend claimed that she sprung fully-formed from Zeus's head. She was one of many daughters of Zeus, and perhaps the most important. She was associated with wisdom, a domain that did not always have a god assigned to it in mythologies, and rarely a woman. Athena was perhaps among the most unique of the Greek gods, even seeming to have a sort of maleness to her that may suggest that she was an older goddess when it came to the relative age of worship. Athens was sacred to Athena, and to the Romans, she was known as Minerva.

Aphrodite

Aphrodite was a goddess of love. When it comes to being a curious god, that is, strange when all the factors are weighed together, Aphrodite gives Athena a run for her money. Aphrodite was a goddess who certainly did not originate with the Greeks. Much of Greek worship came as a result of trade. The Greeks would have been trading with the various groups of the Near East from an early period, and Aphrodite certainly was a goddess who must have been picked up by merchants who had been exposed to the worship of Astarte and other female goddesses of a sensual type in places like Phoenicia and Syria.

Foreign though she may be, Aphrodite had many stories told about her in Greek myth. Whenever there was an element of love or desire in a story, Aphrodite was usually worked in somehow. She played a role in the Trojan War as the goddess that Paris chose to give the apple to, and she was coveted by both god and mortal because of her great beauty. It was said that she washed up naked on a seashell, which is a famous image because of a Renaissance Botticelli painting. Aphrodite was the patroness of the city of Cnidus in Asia Minor, and also of Paphos on Cyprus, where it was said she had been born. In Rome, she was known as Venus.

Ares

Ares was the god of war. As far as war gods go, Ares seems almost peripheral to Greek myth. This is mostly because all Greek gods could be worshipped and praised in war. This was because gods were patrons and patronesses of this city or that, and they would be invoked in war times regardless of whether or not they had an explicitly warlike function. So the Athenians would invoke Athena in war and the Argives would naturally invoke Hera, and so on.

This reality seemed to leave a little role for Ares in Greek life. In Greek myth, however, Ares crops up now and again. He was known for his love (or lust) of Aphrodite, and the sort of menage trois the twain shared with the jealous Hephaestus. Again, this is an example of Greek myth seeming to reflect one of the realities of human life: the infidelity seems to be more human even than monogamy. Ares was the patron of few cities in Ancient Greece, at least as far as the major ones go. In Rome, this god was known as Mars.

Hephaestus

Hephaestus was the blacksmith of the gods and the husband of Aphrodite. As Greek gods go, there is something un-Greek about him. On the other hand, one might say that there was something most Greek about him. If Aphrodite was the foreign harlot who seduced the Greeks into worshipping her, Hephaestus embodied the hapless Greek man who fell for her charms. Where the other Olympian gods were beautiful and generally depicted as being youthful and idealized, Hephaestus (when he was shown) was depicted as being a rather unattractive man.

Though Hephaestus seems like he would be a peripheral character, he does pop up in myths not infrequently.

He is associated with the story of King Minos and the Minotaur, as well as the story of Jason and the Argonauts. As has already been stated, Hephaestus was married to Aphrodite so he often crops up in tales relating to her. There were few major cities devoted to Hephaestus, though shrines devoted to him were not uncommon.

Hades

Hades was a god of a darker shade. He was the god of the underworld, the place where men journeyed to when they died. Hades was not frequently depicted in art, but when he was the artist was sure to imbue him with a macabre character.

It was said that one had to cross the River Styx to enter his land, which required that one first paid the ferryman. For this reason, the Greeks often buried their dead with a coin under the tongue. He was married to Persephone, whom he kidnapped and brought to his land. There were no cities devoted to Hades, and his worship was certainly minute compared to the other gods.

Demeter

Demeter was the goddess of the harvest. She is often depicted in art with an element that suggested grain and agricultural produce, such as a crown of wheat or holding husks of wheat.

She would have been prayed to by men and women who lived in the countryside and who hoped for a bountiful harvest. She also would have been prayed to by people hoping to be delivered from famine. As Greece was not a bountiful land when it came to the soil, Demeter was almost a peripheral goddess compared to similar roles in other societies. Indeed, the Norse had several gods responsible for fertility and the harvest. Indeed, there was an entire group of gods, the Vanir, who were believed to have been old fertility gods that had warred with the primary group of Norse gods (the Aesir). The result was that some of them were recruited to join the Aesir.

The Greeks only had one fertility goddess, although it could be argued that Dionysus was a fertility god of a sort, too. Many cities had shrines to Demeter, and her worship was particularly important in areas where grain growing was of importance, like Ionia in Asia Minor and Thessaly.

Dionysus

Dionysus is another god who appears to have a non-Greek origin. It has been suggested that this god, a son of Zeus, was of Thracian origin. The Thracians were a people who lived on the eastern side of the Black Sea so they would have been far northern neighbors of the Greeks. Greek explorers and colonizers would have come across the Thracians in their attempt to plant colonies in order to secure a constant flow of grain to Greece. the cities of the North Aegean and the Black Sea (especially the cities of Asia Minor) would be very important to the Greeks as a source of food. This is why the defeat of the Persians led to a golden age for the Greeks: cities that produced grain suddenly found themselves free to trade and export as they chose.

Dionysus was the god of wine and reveling. He was associated with Bacchanalian festivals, named after the god's moniker in Latin: Bacchus.

These were orgiastic rites that were supposed to impact the wine crop.

Viticulture was very important in Greece, as well as the Mediterranean culture in general. Dionysus was often invoked by statues or markers at crossroads that featured a bearded man with a phallus pointing up on the front of the marker. Dionysus was worshipped in most Greek cities, including Eleusis, which lay near Athens.

Hermes

Hermes was the messenger of the gods of Mount Olympus. A son of Zeus, he was often depicted with winged sandals, representing the flight that the god took in his role as messenger. Hermes did not belong to the primary group of gods, which included Apollo, Athena, Zeus, and Poseidon, but there were temples devoted to his worship. Indeed, because so much of Greek life depended on the ability to communicate with distant places, the facilitation of that communication necessarily took a place of paramount importance.

This was part of the role that Hermes played. In myth, this god was involved primarily with the gods' communication with man, but in practical life during the golden age of Greek civilization, Hermes was involved with communication in general. So one might pray to Hermes before an important voyage, especially if there was a need for auspicious communication. There were temples dedicated to Hermes throughout the Greek world, and this god was frequently depicted in art. Hermes also was a frequent character encountered in Greek myth.

Artemis

Artemis was an important goddess in Greek myth. Indeed, Artemis was not only an important female divinity but a key divinity in general. Artemis was the goddess of the moon. She was also a huntress and the patroness of hunters. For this reason, Artemis often depicted as a beautiful woman dressed in hunting attire. Another daughter of Zeus, her beauty was enough to arouse the desire of men like Actaeon. But like other goddesses, Artemis was vain. She was one of the contestants in the contest to see which goddess was the most beautiful.
As the goddess of the moon, Artemis's worship was widespread throughout the Greek world. This is a convenient time to talk about another aspect of Greek worship that is important.

We have already spoken about the gods as patrons of cities, but they were also revered for their attributes. So a Norse city might have shrines to many gods, but the Greeks tended to focus their worship on a handful of divinities that were particularly important based on their usage. Greek worship, therefore, had a highly regional character, and some of this had to do with the ethnic groups within the Greek world, like the Ionians, Dorians, Aeolians and the like.

It seems that Artemis was particularly favored in the Eastern cities of the Greek world, particularly in Asia Minor.

Although today we tend to think of the cities of Ionia and other places of Asia Minor as colonies, they had been settled so long by the Classical period that it is almost incorrect to refer to them as such. Cities like Miletus, Ephesus, and Smyrna were just as important as Argos, Thebes, Corinth, and other important regional centers on the Greek mainland.

Hestia

Hestia was the Greek goddess of the hearth. She was also associated with fire. The eldest daughter of Cronys and Rhea, Hestia was, therefore, the elder sister of Zeus, king of the gods. It was not a coincidence that the elder of the Olympian gods was a female goddess associated with life and fire. She seems to represent the old gods and old way of worship that was swept away by the invasion of the Achaeans and Dorians in the Heroic Age.

Hestia was said to love peace, and much modern scholarship has focused on the theory that the earliest gods of the Greeks were peaceable. The claim is that it was later Indo-European speakers, presumably from Asia Minor or the European plain, were warlike and brought with them warlike male gods like Zeus and Apollo. This theory seems like an oversimplification of a more complex theological picture and it is. Even the later Indo-Europeans would have had some female gods, and it stands to reason that the earlier people had male gods to boot.

The fire was something very important to older, less developed people, rendering Hestia an important divinity. The hearth was the fire of the home that kept the members of the family warm and which would have also been used to prepare meals. In Greek tradition, when a member of the family left the home, they would take with them some burning embers from the hearth flame to symbolize the home where they had been reared. Public hearths were kept up in villages and large towns. The fire was used in sacrifices and other public festivals, which prevented this old way of worship and of life from falling into disuse.

Ephesus was the sacred city of Artemis, and its temple was one of the largest in the Greek world. It may seem strange for there to be so much devotion to the moon, as there was for Artemis, but these gods were primarily divinities associated with particular places and their realm of the rule was almost incidental. So while Poseidon might be important to worship because fishermen and sailors needed luck at the sea, Artemis might be worshipped merely because she was associated with Ephesus and the particular devotee happened to be from that city. In Roman myth, Artemis was known as Diana, and she was no less significant to the Romans as she was to the Greeks.

Hera's Jealousy

Hera was a daughter of Cronus and Rhea, making her the sister-wife to Zeus, king of the gods. She reigned as queen of Olympus, but it seemed most of her time was spent chasing after or at least being irritated by her husband Zeus. If there had been video cameras in ancient times, Hera probably would have spent most of her days watching them in order to see what Zeus was up to. It is said by some that Zeus was a poor husband for inciting the jealousy of Hera, but Hera was not much better in her fixation with the activities of her husband.

Although the marriage of Zeus and Hera cannot be said to be a happy one, they remained together and the twain in a way modeled the marriage structure that represented the fundamental unit of ancient Greek civilization. Unfortunately for Hera (or Zeus), there were no divorce agreements available if you were a god living on Mount Olympus. There are many tales of Zeus and just as many about Hera. Hera's jealousy was a common subject in myth. But this story begins with how Zeus and Hera became married. Zeus tricked Hera by taking the form of the cuckoo, a small and harmless bird. The bird was wet and slick and Hera clutched it to her breast to warm it. Zeus instantly transformed back to his natural shape, that is, a man and Hera agreed to marry him.

She would remain faithful to Zeus in spite of his infidelities. It seemed she had little choice. She did not want to end up in Tartarus with the Titans, which seemed to be the fate of anyone who went against the will of Zeus. Zeus was not always successful in his attempts to deceive Hera. In one try, he changed a beautiful maiden called Io into a cow. Hera was not fooled and she demanded the heifer as a gift and sent a monster called Argus to guard it. Hermes lulled Argus to sleep and killed him, but Io was not free. She was pursued by a gadfly that Hera sent all the way to Egypt. There the eyes of Argus were transformed into a peacock where they remain to this day.

Hera was beautiful and therefore was just as deserving of admirers as the women that Zeus pursued. A man called Ephialtes made it his goal to capture Hera. They started an unsuccessful war with the Olympian gods. Another admirer was a certain Ixion. Ixion fell in love with Hera at a banquet, but Zeus tricked him by turning a cloud into the shape of Hera. Ixion made love to the cloud and gave birth to the centaurs, an act for which he was punished by being bound to a wheel of fire.

Hephaestus and Aphrodite

Hephaestus was the lame son of Zeus and Hera. According to some legends, Hephaestus was the son of Hera alone. He was married to Aphrodite, goddess of love, which naturally seems like a mismatch. Aphrodite was beautiful, vivacious, and coveted by many, while there were few women who would have been interested in Hephaestus, who was not as fair as the other gods of Olympus. In any event, Aphrodite was well-known for being unfaithful to Hephaestus. She had many lovers, of which the most famous was perhaps Ares. Other lovers of Aphrodite included Poseidon and Hermes. By Hermes, Aphrodite father Hermaphroditus and, according to some, Eros, who was also known as Cupid (to the Romans, at least). Eros was usually depicted in later art as an infant who accompanies Aphrodite, although in some stories he is mentioned as a young man.

In some accounts, Hephaestus was not married to Aphrodite, but to one of the Three Graces. The workshop of Hephaestus was said to be located under Mount Etna in Italy. Hephaestus, of course, was the Vulcan of the Romans.

Nymphs and Other Creatures

Greek mythology may not be as rife with fantastic characters as Norse myth and legend, but they are there nonetheless.

Most of these peripheral characters had to do with bodies of water, though there were others who were associated with other natural elements of the environment. For example, dryads were spirits associated with trees.

The spirits and characters that will be discussed here are essentially the embodied spirits of physical spaces, even if those spaces were changing (like water). They occupied a liminal space between god and mortal. Although they are not properly termed demigods, they had much in common with this particular group. Demigods were essentially the half-mortal children of the gods, and they typically had a longer lifespan and special accouterments that distinguished them from human beings. Although the same is not true of the naiads, nereids, and others, it is true that these creatures or spirits were believed to basically be immortal when it came to the duration of life, although they could be killed as mortals can.

Nymph is basically the catch-all term for the spirit characters discussed in this portion of the chapter. Nereids and naiads are types of nymphs. Nymphs were generally depicted (and thought of) as beautiful young girls. They were associated with fertility and fecundity.

Many gods and demigods were the children on nymphs, including characters like Achilles.

A nymph was the beautiful young girl associated with (usually) a body of water. A nereid was a nymph associated with the sea, while a naiad was usually associated with a discrete aqueous structure, like a fountain. Although there were no cities or temples associated with nymphs, they frequently appeared in myth and legend. Shrines devoted to important local nymphs would have been common in the Greek world.

Chapter 4: The Children of the Gods

In Greek legend, the children of the gods were usually known as demigods. Many of these became famous heroes. Indeed, most of the heroes of Greek myth were the children of the gods. A review of the names who boarded the Argo with Jason reveals how common it was for the gods to father children and for those children to appear in Greek myth. Unlike other mythologies, it seemed common in Greece for mortal men to claim a godly ancestor. Some of the Argonauts who were the children of gods included:

Adolphus, son of Ares; Calais, son of Boreas, the North Wind; Echion, son of Hermes; Heracles, son of Zeus; Idmon, son of Apollo; Melampus, son of Poseidon; Naupilus, son of Poseidon; Palaemon, son of Hephaestus; Periclymenus, son of Poseidon; Phanus, son of Dionysus; Staphylus, brother to Phanus; Zetes, another son of Boreas.

The Children of Zeus

Zeus, the presiding king of Mount Olympus, had many loves and fathered many children. By Hera, he fathered Ares, Hephaestus, and Hebe. It has been mentioned the claim that Hera might have birthed Hephaestus on her own, but most sources give Zeus as the father. Zeus's first wife was not Hera, but Metis.

Metis became pregnant, but Zeus, in the fashion of his family, swallowed Metis so that a child would not be born who would be greater than himself. This child was Athena, who therefore sprung from the head of Zeus and was the beneficiary of his wisdom.

Zeus had other children besides. By a certain Electra, Zeus was the father of Harmonia. Zeus fathered the Three Graces by Eurynome. Leto was the mother of Apollo and Artemis. Hermes was the son of Zeus by Maia. Mnemosyne was the mother of the Muses, all daughters. Themis, the embodiment of the law, gave birth to several children including the Horae, Eunomia, Dike, the Fates, and Eirene, whose name means peace. Children of Zeus by mortal women include Amphion, Zethus, Perseus, Epaphus, Castor, Pollux (or Polydeuces), Argos (who founded the city of Argos), and Dionysius, who was the son of Semele.

Gods and Demigods

Demigods were usually sired by a father who was a divinity and a mother who was a mortal, nymph, or another non-divine character.
Demigods were given a special name because they often had divine attributes associated with them, such as a fair and

pleasing appearance, long life, better than normal strength, or some other skill that set them apart from the other run of the mill human beings that were encountered in Greek myth and legend.

Greek mythology is unique in setting these characters apart as special. In many other mythologies, the children of gods by mortals are usually just human beings, though in some cases they might be adopted among the gods. As the gods were practically a race apart from human beings it seems strange that they would take such a fancy to mortals as to reproduce with them. There were enough gods around that Zeus, Apollo, and others could have had their pick. Stranger still that the gods seemed not only inclined to procreate with mortals but that the offspring of these unions seemed to be special targets of their attention.

Many important characters of Greek myth are demigods. Obvious examples include Heracles and Perseus.
We have already seen that many of the participants in the journey of Jason to Colchis were also demigods. Why does any of this matter? Well, the demigod seems to concentrate on his person the goal of Greek myth, which was to use the gods to teach Man how to live.

The Greek gods were supposed to set the example of how men should behave and "be," although it was not always a good example. Indeed, the message from the gods seemed to be that man should try his best to be merry at all times, even if it meant inciting the rage of one's wife (we're looking at you, Zeus).

The demigod can be thought as a way in which Greek mythology instructed mortals: "this is how you should be like the gods." It is interesting that the demigods of Greek myth and legend were not unfortunate characters whose lived seemed to represent a lesson on how things can go poorly no matter what one does.
There were no tragic mulattos in the Greek mythos. The demigods were larger than life heroes who overcame the odds to be more like gods than men. Indeed, the gods held all the good cards.
They had super-strength, great wisdom, immortal life, beauty, and a great number of other advantages.
The demigods, on the other hand, were relegated to living on the earth as bastards whose fathers might have been gods or just deadbeats who disappeared. The stories of Perseus, Theseus, Bellerophon, and even heroes like Achilles seemed to be about overcoming the gods, a challenge which the best demigods accomplished adeptly.

Let us take a moment to examine perhaps the most famous demigod of them all: Heracles. Heracles was certainly blessed with strength, but he was also beset with labors that required him to incessantly prove himself. As if being a bastard was not hard enough. He had to beat lions, save himself from lecherous queens, all the while maintaining that sunny Greek demigod demeanor. He could not allow others to see him sweat. One wonders what the point of it all was, and it really was the same point that came from all the demigod's stories. It was the demigod's role to show how Man could be like a god. Man might even be better than god. Gods were seldom punished for their acts of lecherousness or cruelty, but Man usually was. It was this punishment that gave them their humanity, a thing the Greeks understood well. The Greeks were conscious that the lot of Man was hard, but they must have also understood that Man had the blessing of a reward at the end of his labors, a lesson that the twelve labors of Heracles seemed to embody.

The Birth of Heracles

Heracles was the demigod and hero par excellence. He was worshipped as a god in many places, and, indeed, he had been deified by Zeus who is said to have whisked his son away from his funeral pyre. Heracles's mother was a mortal woman called Alcmene.

She was the wife of a certain Amphitryon who lived in Thebes. Both Alcmene and Amphitryon were descendants of the famous hero Perseus. Zeus seduced Alcmene by disguising himself as her husband. At the time, Amphitryon was away at war. Zeus's desire was to father a son who would be a great hero. Amphitryon also wanted to father such a son, and he did when he returned. This son was the half-brother of Heracles and was known as Iphicles.

When he was only an infant, jealous Hera sent two serpents two murder him in his sleep. The jealousy and hatred of the queen of Olympus for the offspring of her husband's infidelity knew no bounds.

But the baby already showed signs of his godly origin. The infant Heracles strangled the snakes sent by Hera with his bare hands. Some said that it was Amphitryon who sent the serpents, as he was angered that his queen had fathered a child by another, even if that other was the king of the gods.

The Amazons

All right, so the Amazons were not children of the gods, nor where they demigods (or demi goddesses), but they have to be discussed somewhere. The Amazons were female warriors who were said to live at the "edge of the world." To some, this meant Asia Minor, while others placed their locale in Africa. The Amazons were under the special protection of Artemis, a goddess who regarded the hunt and all wild things as sacred. As the Amazons were somewhat wild, at least in the uncivilized fashion in which they lived, it seems sensible that they would be under her protection.

The Amazons were said to kidnap men and use them as studs to sire strong children.

They only selected the best men for this task. Naturally, patriarchal Greek society viewed this practice (and the women who engaged in it) with horror.

It has been argued by some that the Amazon myth may have originated with warlike Scythian warriors who lived on the Russian steppes.

They may have had warrior women in their ranks, providing ample imaginative fodder to Ancient Greek audiences who seemed inclined to believe everything.

The Amazons were not peripheral in Greek myth, appearing in a number of legends. In particular, they are associated with one of the labors of Heracles. The Amazons were ruled by a queen, of which the most famous was Hippolyta. This race of warrior women was said to live on a mountain called Themiscyra. The Amazons ran into Heracles when this hero stole the girdle of Queen Hippolyta. Hippolyta was subsequently bested by Theseus and ended up bearing him a son. This son was known as Hippolytus. Another Amazon queen was Penthesilea who fought on the Trojan side in the Trojan War. She would be slain in battle by Achilles.

There were many legends about the Amazons. Some writers asserted that the warrior women cut off one of their breasts to allow better use of their bow arm. Though this tale is commonly told, it has been portrayed in ancient art.

Chapter 5: Theseus and Other Heroes

The Ancient Greek world was rife with the tales of heroes and their adventures. Just as the gods had their regional affiliations and cities of devotion, so too were the heroes revered in the lands where they hailed from. Theseus was revered in Athens, where he ruled as king. Perseus was revered throughout the Greek world, but especially in Argos. Heracles was also widely worshipped, but Thebes in Boetia was his native land. Jason and the Argonauts were revered in Thessaly and other regions related to the tale.

Learning the tales of the Greek heroes allows the reader to understand those qualities the Greeks respected and sought to encourage among the populace. Today, we might take note the heroes of legend are exclusively male, and this, of course, is because the Greek idea of the perfect human being was generally a handsome and strong male figure. One can appreciate this in the devotion that Apollo received throughout the Greek world. He was not only the god of the sun, but he also embodied the ideal male characteristics, including the internal ones.

This fixation on an idealized male image is also seen in the artistic interpretation of the heroes and their lives. Even in ancient times, the image of a muscle-bound Heracles was popular in art, including the sort of ceramic ware that would have been common in the houses of the people. But even highly-specialized images like that of Perseus holding the head of Medusa was common in ancient times and received an artistic revival in the 18th and 19th centuries. What this does is tell us how the heroes were perceived: as larger than life characters not unlike the gods.

This fixation on heroes was important in Greek society. This hero worship can be said to be part of the basis of Greek civilization. Male-centered culture started out in the aristocratic prep school of the ephorate, where young men wrestled in the gymnasium and received lessons in philosophy, and it continued as those young men eventually served the time in the war and finally became members of the democracies or oligarchies that existed in their state. This hero worship was always male because power in these societies was exclusively male. So what sort of characteristics were important in the future leaders of Greek cities like Athens, Thebes, Corinth, and Sparta? An examination of the tales of Theseus, Perseus, and Jason will help to answer that question.

The Adventures of Theseus

Theseus was the main hero of Athens, and he had many adventures. Theseus was the son of King Aegeus of Athens by Aethra, who was the princess of a city called Troezen. Troezen was located on the Pelopenessus, and Pittheus ruled as king. Aegeus had come to Troezen as a young man. He fathered a son with Aethra and hid his sandals and sword beneath a rock. He told Aethra to instruct her son to come to him in Athens when he was strong enough to lift the rock and claim the items beneath it. Theseus did this when he was 16, then venturing to Athens to lay claim to his birthright as the king's son, partaking in many adventures along the way. Some of these stories are dramatized in the book *The King Must Die* by Edith Hamilton. Theseus was most famous for his dealings with the Minotaur, which rank among the most well-known and significant of Greek myths.

Before his encounter with the Minotaur, Theseus had to deal with Medea, his father's wife. She was a sorceress who instantly recognized who Theseus was before he revealed himself. Medea attempted to serve Theseus poisoned wine, but before he drank it the boy revealed the gifts that his father had hid under the rock in Troezen. Aegeus dashed the cup of poisoned wine away just in time and embraced his heir. Medea fled from Athens with her own son in tow.

The story of Theseus and the Minotaur begins with the yearly tribute that Athens had to pay to Crete. This tribute was in the form of young boys and girls that Athens had to send to Crete to serve King Minos. Although much of myth was certainly invented by the storytellers, this part of the story at least may have the ring of truth. The Cretans would have been a regional superpower long before their cousins in mainland Greece were. Demanding tribute in the form of slave women and children was not uncommon; it was even practiced by the Turks as late as the 19th century.

Indeed, even Theseus himself has been proposed as a man who lived rather than a mere figure of legend. Theseus was likely a king in very distant times whose life became encapsulated in the legends of cities like Athens and other places. The same is believed to be true of Heracles, who was also likely a king or great man who lived and only later became a demigod.

But back to the story of Theseus and the Minotaur. Theseus was determined to end the practice of Athenian children being sent to Crete so he went with the yearly donation to Crete. When the ship reached Crete, Theseus and the others were eventually taken to see King Minos and his daughter, Ariadne.

This story has been highly fictionalized in Hamilton's work, although it makes for a good read. In the book, much discussion is had about the Minotaur, who in the myths is really just a man with the head of a bull. His name in Greek meant "bull of Minos" (that is, the king of Crete in the myths).

It was time for the seven boys and seven girls of Athens to be sacrificed to the Minotaur. The Minotaur lived in a labyrinth that it was impossible to escape from. Any victim who entered the labyrinth would be unable to escape alive. But Theseus was fortunate as Princess Ariadne had fallen in love with him, Ariadne gave Theseus a ball of string that he could use to find his way out of the labyrinth. Theseus entered the maze to find the creature, and he unwound the string in order to have a pathway back out. After a fierce battle, Theseus slew the bull and used the string to make his way out. Theseus took Ariadne back with him to Athens, but he later abandoned her on the island of Naxos. This last is part of a myth that is nearly as famous as the story of the Minotaur.

The Adventures of Perseus

Perseus ranks with Theseus as among the most important of Greek heroes. He was the son of Danae by Zeus. Danae was the princess of Argos, daughter of King Acrisius.

It had been prophesied by an oracle that Acrisius would die by Danae's son so Acrisius locked her in a room in a high tower to prevent her from being impregnated.

But Zeus visited her in a shower of golden rain, and after nine months she bore Perseus. But Acrisius was not done. He locked both mother and child in a wooden box and sent them afloat on the sea. A fisherman called Dictys spotted the chest and rescued the twain. They were taken to the court of King Polydectes who lived on Seriphos, an island in the Aegean. When Perseus was older, Polydectes fell in love with the beautiful Danae and desired to marry her. To get Perseus out of the way, he sent him on a quest to bring back the head of the gorgon, Medusa. Meanwhile, Danae took refuge at a temple on the island.

Medusa was a monster who had the power to turn her victims to stone. Her tale was told in the film *The Clash of the Titans*, which has been remade. Although Perseus stood little chance against the gorgon Medusa the gods were on his side. Athena, who had been the one to turn Medusa from a beautiful maiden into a monster, was on the side of Perseus. She told Perseus he must never look directly at Medusa's face. She gave him a highly-polished shield, which he could use as a mirror. From Hermes, Perseus received a sickle and a bag in which to carry the gorgon's head. He also received a pair of winged sandals. Finally, Hermes told Perseus where he could find the Graea, the Gray Women, who knew how to find Medusa.

The Graea were old women who had only one eye in which to see and one tooth. They must share these things, constantly passing them around among the three of them. Perseus took the eye and promised only to give it back if they told him where Medusa was. Perseus went to the designated place and used the shield as a mirror to see where Medusa was. He used the weapons he had been given to cut off her head, and then he placed it in the bag he had been given by Hermes. From Medusa's blood, Pegasus, the winged horse, was born.

Perseus used Pegasus to get back to Seriphos. On the way, he saw a princess chained to a rock. She was Andromeda, princess of Ethiopia.

She was the daughter of King Cepheus of Ethiopia and Queen Cassiopeia. Andromeda was tied to the rock because she was to be sacrificed to a sea monster. This monster was known as The Kracken in film. Perseus rescued her and slew the monster, using Medusa's head to turn the monster into stone. Perseus went on to marry Andromeda. Later, the hero returned to Seriphos where he turned King Polydected to stone. Perseus went to attend games at Larissa. He threw a discus which went awry, killing a man in the audience. That man was Acrisius, his grandfather, thus fulfilling the prophecy that the oracle had told so many years before.

Jason and the Argonauts

Jason was the last of the three great heroes of Greek myth, excluding Heracles. He was the son of Aeson, who was a king in Thessaly, in Northern Greece. Jason's father was overthrown by his brother, Pelias, who threatened to kill anyone who challenged his claim to the throne. Jason was smuggled away to safety and placed in the care of a friendly centaur called Chiron. Jason as a man returned to lay claim to his kingdom. On the way, he helped an old woman cross a river. This woman was Hera in disguise and in gratitude, this goddess would always be the supporter of Jason in his exploits.

In helping the woman, Jason lost one of his sandals. Pelias had been warned to be wary of a stranger coming to town wearing one sandal. When he saw Jason, he knew that this was the prophecy fulfilled. To protect his throne, Pelias sent him on a quest to gain the Golden Fleece. he knew that it would be impossible for Jason to accomplish this. But Jason had the aid of the goddesses Hera and Athena. They helped him arrange for the ship Argo to be built. He recruited fifty warriors to go with him. These warriors included Heracles, Castor and Pollux, Orpheus, and Atalanta. They sailed to the land of Colchis on the Black Sea, and after many adventures, they reached this land of the Golden Fleece.

When they reached Colchis, the king forced them to accomplish tasks before he would help them. But Medea, the king's daughter, and a sorceress fell in love with him and offered to help. She gave him the power to defeat fire-breathing bulls, and she gave him advice on how to defeat the warriors that had sprung from dragons' teeth. Medea took Jason to where the Golden Fleece was. It was guarded by a dragon, but they used a potion to place the dragon into slumber. With the dragon asleep, Jason was able to gain the fleece.

After they left Colchis, the Argonauts were pursued by Medea's brother as well as warriors. Medea killed her brother and cut his body into pieces.

This would give them time as her father would have to stop to gather up the pieces and bury his son. They returned to Thessaly where Medea convinced the daughters of Pelias to cut him into pieces, too. She told them that if they put him into a stew he would come back to life. Of course, he did not, and Jason and Medea had to flee Thessaly for Corinth. There, Jason abandoned Medea for Glauca, the daughter of the king of Corinth. Medea dispatched Glauca by giving her a dress that was laced with poison, which killed her. Medea, too, killed Jason's sons. Then she had to flee to Athens to the court of King Aegeus, the father of Theseus.

Historian Robert Graves has provided a well-researched, exhaustive list of the men and women who served with Jason aboard the Argo. This list, of course, included Heracles, the most famous hero in Greek myth, as well as Argus, who designed and built the Argo. The names of the men and women who traveled with Jason aboard the Argo to Colchis to recover the golden fleece are:

Acastus
Actor, of Phocis
Admetus, of Pherae
Amphiaraus, of Argos
Antaeus, of Samos
Argus, shipbuilder
Ascalaphus, demigod, son of Ares

Asterius, of Pelopia

Atalanta, a huntress

Augeias, a native of Elis

Butes, a native of Athens

Caeneus, a Lapith

Calais, son of Boreas, the North Wind

Canthus, of Euboea

Castor, along with Pollux or Polydeuces, one of the Dioscuri

Cepheus, son of Aleus of Arcadia

Corionis, another Lapith

Echion, demigod, son of Hermes

Erginus, a native of Miletus

Euphemus

Euryalus

Heracles, demigod, son of Zeus

Hylas, friend, and companion to Heracles

Idas, of Messene

Idmon, demigod, son of Apollo and native of Argos

Iphicles

Iphitus, of Mycenae

Laertes, of Argos

Lynceus, a brother to Idas

Melampus, demigod, son of Poseidon

Meleager, a native of Calydon

Mopsus, yet another Lapith

Naupilus, demigod, son of Poseidon and native of Argos

Oileus, brother to Ajax, a well-known hero

Orpheus, a poet

Palaemon, demigod, son of Hephaestus

Peleus, a member of the race of Myrmidons

Peneleos, a native of Boetia

Periclymenus, demigod, son of Poseidon

Phalerus, a native of Athens

Phanus, demigod, a native of Crete and son to Dionysus

Poeas, a native of Magnesia

Polydeuces (or Pollux), brother to Castor and one of the Dioscuri

Polyphemus, a native of Arcadia

Staphylus, a native of Crete and brother to Phanus

Typhus, the ship's helmsman on the Argo

Zetes, another son of Boreas

Chapter 6: Tales of Zeus

As king of the gods, there were naturally many myths and legends about Zeus. Zeus was the father figure who presided over the affairs of both god and Man from his perch on Mount Olympus. That being said, Greek myth was pretty clear that most of Zeus's role in the affairs of Man was of an amorous nature. If Zeus was not chasing after this fair maid or that, he was trying to fix the mess that Hera's jealousy had created. As everything in Greek mythology seemed to be symbolic, perhaps Zeus symbolized the creative power of men, a power that was often most visible in their propensity for... well, procreation.

Zeus and Ganymede

Zeus had many loves. Most of them were men, but not all of them were. Ganymede was a beautiful youth, usually described as being a prince of Troy. He was the great-grandson of Dardanus, the founder of Troy and the namesake for the Dardanelles, part of the passage from the Aegean Sea to the Black Sea.
Enamored of the youth, Zeus spirited him off to Mount Olympus to be the cupbearer to the gods.

Some say that he accomplished this by taking the form of wind while others said Zeus did this by transforming himself into an apple. This mythological event was a popular inspiration for art throughout the Greco-Roman period.

Zeus and Leda

The myth of Zeus and Leda was one of many that were immortalized in art. Leda was the beautiful daughter of the king of Aetolia, a region of Greece. She was the wife of the king of Sparta, a certain Tyndareus. Zeus became enamored of her and desired to have his way with her. Zeus took the form of a swan in order to seduce her. She mated with Zeus while he was in the form of a swan and subsequently laid an egg. From this egg hatched Helen (known as Helen of Troy) and Polydeuces, one of the Dioscuri. Leda also sired Castor (another of the Dioscuri) and Clytemnestra by her husband Tyndareus. These last came by normal, vaginal birth.

Zeus and Leto

Leto was most famous for being the mother of the important gods Apollo and Artemis. Leto is also important, mythologically speaking, for being one of the many conquests of Zeus. It was said that Leto was known for being very gentle. In particular, the poet Hesiod described her thus.

Because Leto had lain with Zeus, she earned the ire of Hera, who was prone to tormenting those whom Zeus had chosen to rest his eyes upon.

Leto was being relentlessly pursued by Hera, who was therefore forced to wander from city to city looking for shelter. She finally found refuge on the small island of Delos. It was here that she would give birth to the twin gods Apollo and Artemis. Legend said that it had been Artemis who was born first. Artemis instantly grew to be a woman and assisted her mother in giving birth to Apollo. Apollo followed shortly after. Because Delos was the birthplace of Apollo, it became a famous place throughout the Greek world and a site of refuge during both Greek and Roman times.

Chapter 7: Tales of Apollo

Apollo was one of the more important gods of Mount Olympus. He was the god of the sun and was worshipped all over Greece. Indeed, few of the Olympian gods had more stories told about them than Apollo. Although Zeus edges Apollo out somewhat because of his numerous loves (and the numerous forms he took to seduce the women involved in these loves), Apollo perhaps is a close second when it comes to the number of myths and legends. Apollo sired several important children, and he was also the most famous oracle in the Greek world: the oracle of Delphi.

The Children of Apollo

Apollo loved many beautiful women, not all of whom fared well. Apollo loved the nymph Daphne, who did everything she could to save herself from the god's touch. She was transformed into a laurel tree, which the god made his sacred emblem. Corionis was not more fortunate. Corionis, too, was loved by Apollo, but she deserted him after giving birth to Aesculapius, the god of medicine and healing. Artemis revenged herself for this affront to her brother by killing her in a hail of arrows. The infant son of Apollo was snatched away to be raised by Hermes.

Apollo had a son called Aristaeus by the nymph Cyrene. But perhaps the most famous son of Apollo in Greek myth was Phaeton. Technically, Phaeton was the son of Helios, the embodiment of the sun. Helios was originally a distinct god who eventually was united with Apollo as Apollo Helios. The favored place of Helios or Apollo Helios was the island of Rhodes.

Phaeton was the son of Apollo Helios, but his friends would not believe him. He asked his father to let him drive his chariot and Apollo reluctantly agreed. Phaeton was not able to control the horse to drive the chariot and he eventually devastated the land that became Libya. Zeus hurled a thunderbolt at him and the young man was turned into a swan. He would live out the rest of his life among the Heliades, who were his sisters. They had been turned into weeping willows because they mourned the death of their brother. This was one of many stories told in the *Metamorphoses* of Ovid.

Apollo and Cassandra

Cassandra is famous as a princess of Troy, but she was well-known for the wrong reasons. This princess was known because no one would believe her prophecies.
She had Apollo to thank for this. Apollo had fallen in love with the beautiful daughter of King Priam of Troy.

He gave her the gift of foretelling the future, but she disappointed him by falling in love with another. Apollo punished her by taking away her ability to persuade, leaving her only her skill for prophecy. Therefore, Cassandra was relegated to telling startling accurate prophecies that no one believed.

The Oracle of Delphi

Delphi was regarded by the Greeks as the center of the world. There was placed here a navel stone. Delphi was the place where the infamous Oracle presided. She was able to speak the words of the divinities of Mount Olympus, and her prophecies always came true. Delphi was sacred to Apollo, but it was believed that it had previously been sacred to another, namely Gaia, the earth goddess and grandmother of Zeus.

When Delphi was sacred to Gaia it was called Pytho. It is from the name Pytho that the Pythian Games originated. The Oracle of Apollo was also called the Pythia. The Pythian Games were among the most important games in the Greek world. Many came to compete in the games, just as many came to seek the knowledge of the Pythia. The name also references the Python who was a snake that Apollo vanquished. The ruins of the temple of Apollo can still be seen at Delphi, which rests on the slopes of the famed Mount Parnassus.

Laocoon

Laocoon was a priest of Apollo whose death has been immortalized in art. A popular statue group from the Hellenistic Age displayed the manner in which this man died, and a copy from the Roman period remains to be appreciated in the present day. Laocoon was a Trojan priest who unfortunately earned the ire of the god Apollo. Some stories place him as one of the many sons of Priam. Laocoon broke his vow of celibacy by marrying and proceeding to sire children with his wife.

Laocoon was chosen by the Trojans to make sacrifices to the god Poseidon after the previous priest died. Before beginning his priestly duties, Laocoon warned King Priam to "beware of Greeks bearing gifts," referring to the Trojan horse that the Greeks were hiding in to sneak into the city. Laocoon went to the altar with his sons Antipas and Thymbreus. While standing at the altar of Poseidon, two sea serpents rose from the sea wrapped their bodies around the three and killed them. The enormous serpents had been sent by Apollo to punish Laocoon.

Apollo and Hyacinthus

The Greek gods loved beautiful things, especially beautiful women.

Their roving eyes paid special attention to the aesthetic sights that the world of humans had to offer.

Zeus was infamous for this, but Apollo was also guilty of this wandering eye. Hyacinthus was one of the loves of Apollo. He would end his life as a flower, one that still exists today.

Hyacinthus was usually described as a prince of Sparta, the son of King Amyclas and Queen Diomede. Others describe Hyacinthus as being the son of Pierus and Clio, the latter one of the Muses. Hyacinthus was killed by the West Wind, Zephyrus. A discus was sent flying by the West Wind and it struck the young man in the head. Apollo saved the youth that he had loved by transforming him into a pleasant-smelling flower: the hyacinth.

Chapter 8: The Twelve Labors of Heracles

Heracles was arguably the greatest hero of Greek legend. He certainly was the most famous. Though his feats bring comparisons to others like Perseus and Theseus, neither of these two could claim the twelve labors that Heracles had to overcome. The source of his labors was a punishment laid upon him by the gods. Heracles was prone to fits of madness, not unlike the "Berzerker" rages that Norsemen were prone to in the sagas. It was during such a rage that Heracles slew not only his brother's children but his own.

Heracles's punishment was to serve the king of Argos, a certain Eurystheus. Like Heracles's parents, this king was descended from the hero Perseus. As part of his atonement for his crimes, Heracles was bidden to complete twelve labors over a time period of twelve years. These twelve labors were regarded as impossible; they certainly would have been impossible for an ordinary man. In spite of the practical impossibility of his task, Heracles managed to best them all, making him a permanent fixture as the greatest of men (though he technically was a demigod since he was the son of Zeus). As Heracles is sometimes depicted where a lion's skin, it should come as no surprise that his first task was to overcome the Nemean lion.

First Labor: The Nemean Lion

The first labor involved the besting of a lion known as the Nemean lion. This lion was so-called because it lived at a place called Nemea near Corinth. This area would later become the site of a famous athletic competition held every two years called the Nemean Games. This was part of a cycle of games that the best athletes in the historical period attended (a cycle which naturally included the Olympic Games, the most famous games in the Greek world).

The Nemean lion was an enormous creature who was the offspring of Selene, the embodiment of the moon. The Nemean lived in a cave that could only be entered by one of two ways. After many attempts to best the lion, Heracles came up with an idea. He would seal off one of the entrances, allowing only one route of egress. Then, Heracles battled the lion and strangled it with his bare hands, much as he had the serpents in his crib when he was a babe. It was said that the two mouths of the cave of the Nemean lion embodied the twelve labors themselves, which had a beginning and an end.

Second Labor: The Hydra of Lernea

Hydras were monsters with multiple heads. A head regrew each time one was lopped off, making the hydra a seemingly unbeatable flow.

Indeed, the Hydra of Lernea sounds like the worst boss in a 1990s Nintendo game.

At this point, Heracles was accompanied by his friend Iolaus, who would be around for many of the labors. Iolaus helped Heracles by burning the stumps of the hydra's heads after Heracles lopped them off to prevent the heads from growing back.

With his heads unable to regrow, the hydra slowly was defeated until Heracles was finally able to vanquish the terrible beast. But this labor was not done. Heracles dipped his arrows in the blood of the hydra, thus fortifying them with a deadly poison.

Third Labor: The Wild Boar of Erymanthus

The wild boar was a vicious animal that inhabited an area of fields and woods. At the time of this labor, the fields of the Wild Boar of Erymanthus were covered with snow. Heracles hunted the animal through fields that were inches deep with snow. Heracles decided that the best way to best the animal was to capture it and deliver it rather than merely to slay it and give Eurystheus of Argos the proof of his victory. Perhaps Heracles real goal was to scare the king as the gods and heroes were known for being playful.

So Heracles brought the Wild Boar of Erymanthus alive back to King Eurystheus of Argos.

It was said that the king was so frightened by the sight of the famous wild boar that he hid so as not to be harmed. He hid in a bronze jar large enough for a man where Heracles found him.

Fourth Labor: The Hind of Ceryneia

You may be starting to see a pattern. The earlier labors of Heracles seem to involve the besting of large or fabulous creatures, which seems little more than an exercise in brute strength on the part of the Theban hero. The Hind of Ceryneia was so-called because it lived in Arcadia, which is a forested land in the center of the Peloponnese peninsula. This was a large peninsula that essentially covered the southern half of Greece. On this peninsula were located several cities, including Sparta, Argos, and Elis. Corinth was located on the isthmus that connected this peninsula to mainland Greece. The main cities of Arcadia were called Tegea and Mantinea.

It was said that the Hind of Ceryneia was a beautiful animal: a deer. The task of Heracles was to capture this hind. Slaying it might have angered the goddess Artemis, so merely capturing it would spare the hero this goddess's wrath.
The deer ran very swiftly, making it difficult for the hero to capture it.

It was said to have feet made of bronze and antlers the color of gold metal. The hind was so swift that Heracles was only able to capture it after a year of trying. He took the hind to Eurystheus unharmed.

Fifth Labor: The Stymphalian Birds

There is something truly frightening about birds, and the Stymphalian birds were no exception. These were birds of bronze, with their claws, beaks, and wings all made of this powerful metal. The Stymphalian Birds had an appetite for the flesh of humans. The birds were so numerous that their shape blotted out the sun when they all took flight together. Heracles's first obstacle here was to find a way to frighten them. The second part was then to cause them to never to return to the lands they ravaged again. Heracles managed to frighten the birds by using a giant bronze rattle to create a horrible noise. Heracles was aided in the making of this rattle by the goddess Athena, who apparently was not overly fond of birds (or at least not birds of this sort). The rattle worked and the Stymphalian Birds flew off, never to be heard from again.

It was said that the healing powers attributed to Heracles were associated with his feats in this labor.
Heracles healed the land by getting rid of fearsome animals that plagued it.

It was said that Heracles had the ability to heal ague or fever. As fevers were poorly understood at this time, the ability to heal them was enough to gather around one many devotees. Also, the acquisition of fever in Greece was associated with living in marshy areas where there were a number of large birds predominating, like ibises and cranes. The Stymphalian birds may have been modeled on these birds associated with Egyptian art.

Sixth Labor: The Augean Stables

The midway point of Heracles's labors was one of the more interesting ones. Heracles was tasked with cleaning the stables of King Augeus. Heracles only had one day to accomplish this labor. Augeus was king of Elis, which was located on the Western end of the Peloponnesus. This was the area of Greece where the Olympian Games would later be held.

Heracles had a tall order in cleaning these pestilent stables, but he managed to accomplish the task. He did this by ingeniously diverting the course of two rivers.
These rivers lay nearby to the stables of King Augeus, and by diverting them he was able to wash the stables of their dung and disease without having to handle each stall or horse individually.

This labor has led to a euphemism which refers to the task of having to clean an area that is dirty, even if the dirt represents a religious or moral problem.

Seventh Labor: The Cretan Bull

Crete was a land associated with bulls. This is because the Cretans had perfected the art of bull dancing since the Minoan period. Indeed, some of the earliest artists to be found in modern-day Greece comes from the Minoan period on Crete. At the time of this labor, a bull was terrorizing the island. Heracles's task was to capture this bull and return with it in hand to mainland Greece. This bull was later killed by Theseus, who was known for his prowess against bulls. In besting this labor, Heracles managed to accomplish one of the tasks that were associated with heroes. This sort of test had also been imposed on Jason and Theseus.

Eighth Labor: The Horses of Diomedes

This particular Diomedes lived in Thrace. His horses were mild mares whom Diomedes fed with human flesh. Monsters that ate the flesh of people was a common trope in Greek legend. Although horses that dined on flesh was a first. Heracles bested this task by first slaying Diomedes and then feeding the horses with his flesh.

After this act, the horses were said to behave in a more tame, malleable fashion than they had previously. Taming of horses by a hero was seen as a crucial rite in many early European societies, and there were even echoes of it in the New World (after horses had been introduced by the Spanish).

Ninth Labor: The Girdle of the Amazon

Hippolyta was the most famous queen of the Amazons. According to one legend, she would later be defeated by Theseus of Athens by whom she gave birth to a son named Hippolytus. Heracles's task here was to obtain the girdle of Hippolyta. King Eurystheus intended to use this Amazonian girdle as a gift for his daughter, the princess. According to one recount of this labor, Hippolyta became enamored of Heracles and gave him the girdle voluntarily. It makes sense, as Amazonian women were said to have a hankering for men who were strong and masculine as Heracles was.

Tenth Labor: Geryon's Cattle

Geryon was the name of a monster with three heads. Unlike other monsters, however, Geryon kept a herd of cattle for which he was quite famous in Greece. This story has the echoes of the various stories about giants in Norse mythology, but we digress.

Eurystheus was one of those who envied the multi-headed monster his cattle, and it was the labor of Heracles to obtain these cattle.

Heracles was expected to steal the cattle, an ancient custom, which he did deftly. Apparently, it was not common in early Europe for men to steal cattle and then use the earnings from a cattle ride to pay a bride price for a new spouse.

Eleventh Labor: The Theft of Cerberus

Cerberus was the famous hound that guarded the entrance to Tartarus, the underworld. Cerberus was a three-headed dog whose job was to prevent people from getting into the underworld who were not meant to be there. Heracles's labor was to bring the hound back to Argos, although Eurystheus never expected Heracles to succeed in the task. Succeeding where would mean traveling to the land of the dead, making it in and out alive, and then returning to the land of the living.

Fortunately for Heracles, he had some divine help in this labor. The gods Athena and Hermes offered to help. With their help, Heracles managed to best both Hades, the god of the underworld, and Cerberus. He took the three-headed dog back to King Eurystheus, who again jumped inside of a bronze jar to hide. He was not a particularly courageous king, hence the need to make Heracles do all the heavy lifting.

Twelfth Labor: The Apples of the Hesperides

The Hesperides were the daughters of Atlas. Atlas was the Titan who was damned to carry the sky on his shoulders for leading the Titans against the Olympians. The golden apples of the Hesperides were actually the property of Hera, wife of Zeus. It was the job of a dragon called Ladon to guard the apples against anyone who might try to take them. Atlas was the only one who knew where the orchard of apples lies so Heracles went to him for information. Heracles offered to carry the sky on his own shoulders if Atlas would fetch some of the apples. According to some legends, after Atlas returned Heracles tricked him into taking the sky back on his shoulders. Others say that Atlas was freed by Heracles.

Chapter 9: Lighter Tales of Greek Gods and Heroes

Not all of the tales of Greek myth and legend had to do with the main gods like Zeus and Apollo or better-known heroes like Perseus, Theseus, and Jason. The Greek world was rife with stories of this figure or that who may have had a regional significance, or a minor role in the larger picture of Greek mythology. One of the things that set Greek mythology apart is the profusion of stories, and in this chapter, we will explore some of the picturesque if not essential stories of Greek myth. Of course, there are many stories like this and in this chapter, we only have time for a small selection.

Oedipus and his Children

Oedipus, though not a god or a hero, was one of the more important figures in Greek myth.

Oedipus is particularly known for his treatment in Greek drama, and it is interesting to examine how important he would be as a figure if the Greek dramatists had not had such a go at his life. Oedipus's name meant "swollen foot" in Geek. He was the son of the king of Thebes, Laius, by his wife Jocasta. He would be the father of several children; namely, Antigone, Eteocles, Ismene, and Polynices.

Laius had heard the pronouncement of the oracle that his son would kill his father and marry his mother so he abandoned his infant boy on a hillside. In Ancient Greece, it was common to abandon unwanted children (or children who could not be cared for) in this fashion. Before Laius abandoned his son, he pierced his son's foot, which is why Oedipus was given the name of the swollen foot. A shepherd found the babe and took him to the king of Corinth who raised him. Oedipus heard the story that he would kill his father and marry his mother so he left Corinth, thinking that the king and queen of Corinth were his real parents.

Oedipus ended up meeting Laius at a crossroads. They had an altercation and Oedipus slew him. he then went to Thebes where he successfully answered a riddle invented by the Sphinx. As a result, he won the hand of the queen of Thebes, who was his mother Jocasta.

He married her unknowing that she was his mother, and he inadvertently fulfilled the prophecies of the Sphinx. When he learned the truth, Oedipus blinded himself as he could no longer face reality. He went to exile in Attica while his children battled each other for control of Thebes. This is the story of the Seven Against Thebes. Oedipus was accompanied by his daughter Antigone who faithfully escorted her blind father in his wanderings.

Artemis and Actaeon

The story of Artemis and Actaeon was an important one in the compendium of tales about Artemis. It reveals her character as a goddess and sets her apart as being quite different from Aphrodite, for example. Actaeon was a handsome hunter, the grandson of Cadmus and the son of a certain Autonoe. He was hunting with his ferocious dogs in the woods when he had the misfortune to come across the nude Artemis bathing in a river in the wood. He could not tear himself away even though he knew there would be consequences of seeing the goddess naked. By the time he looked away, it was too late. The goddess revered herself for the affront by setting the man's own dogs on him. The hunting dogs tore Actaeon to pieces.

The Myth of Arachne

Arachne was a princess of Lydia who was well-known for her skills at the loom. Onlookers said that she must have been trained by Athena herself, and the proud girl offered to compete against the goddess in a competition. Athena, annoyed, accepted the invitation. The maiden was so good at weaving than Athena could find no fault with it. The maiden had woven scenes of the gods disporting themselves in their happy revels. Athena ripped the work apart and dashed the loom. Arachne wanted to hang herself, but Athena turned her instead into a spider, cursed to always revel in the cobwebs that are the weaving work of the spider.

Cupid and Psyche

Cupid, known as Eros to the Greeks, was the god of love. We call him Cupid here as that is the name by which he is most well-known. He represented the chaotic side of love and for this reason, he was both feared and worshipped by his devotees. It is not clear who his parents were in myth, but he is usually thought of as the son of Aphrodite. His father was either Zeus, Ares, or Hephaestus, depending on which ancient source you consult.

Psyche was the most beautiful princess in the world. Aphrodite, in a rage, ordered her son to punish the girl by making her fall in love with someone embarrassing.

Instead, Cupid accidentally scratched himself with his own arrow and therefore fell in love. He carried the princess off to a palace and subsequently married her, but he did not reveal who he was. The girl was commanded never to look at his face, a commandment which she obeyed, but she fell in love with him anyway. But one day, the sisters of Psyche persuaded her to try and see her face. She lit a lamp and saw the beautiful form of the sleeping young man. In an instant, all the beautiful surroundings that had been wrought for her disappeared. Aphrodite hounded Psyche all over the Greek world until Eros convinced Zeus to make her immortal. The god consented and the wedding of Eros (Cupid) and Psyche was lavishly celebrated on Olympus.

Chapter 10: The Trojan War

The Trojan War was a defining event in Greek mythology and Greek history. Although it is impossible to know whether the primary actors in this drama were men and women who actually lived it is certain the Greeks and Romans regarded them as real, even intertwining the events of the conflict into their own history. The prime example of this is the descent that the Romans traced through to Aeneas, who left Ilium for Italy after the Trojan War.

Like everything else in Greek mythology, the Trojan conflict was filled with symbolism. A common motif in Greek mythology was the idea that pride was a sin that would often lead to the downfall of Man. Men and women were often punished for their pride against the gods, as stories like that of Arachne, Oedipus, and others demonstrate. The prophecies spoken by the oracles were gods will be transmitted to men, and those who refused to obey them would find that all their efforts only served to bring the prophecy into action.

The question then becomes what the Trojan conflict was meant to symbolize.
There was an element of pride in this conflict, too.

The Greek leaders were too proud to unite and defeat the Trojans, forcing them to spend ten years on a conflict that could have been won in a year. Individual Greek warriors like Achilles also displayed pride, which led to their downfall. The Trojans, too, were proud in their attempt to circumvent the will of the gods who seemed to have marked the city of Troy for destruction. Finally, the beauty of Helen was found to be a blessing rather than a curse, resulting in the downfall not only of the Trojans but of most of the Greeks.

The Judgment of Paris

Helen sits at the center of the Trojan conflict, but the story really begins with Paris. Paris was a prince of Troy, a large city on the Western coast of Turkey. This city had been buried for centuries with its precise location unknown until an architect called Schliemann discovered it. The Trojans were not Greeks, although in the myths they seem equivalent to the Greeks, worshipping the same gods and engaging in the same general practices that the Greeks engaged in.

Eris, the goddess of discord, was angered that she had not been given an invitation to the wedding of Peleus and Thetis, who were the parents of Achilles. Out of spite, Eris dropped a golden apple into the wedding feast.

It was inscribed with the words: "To the most beautiful." This naturally led to a quarrel between the goddesses Aphrodite, Athena, and Hera, each of whom believed themselves to be the most beautiful. In some versions of the story, Athena is replaced with Artemis. These goddesses asked Zeus to choose among them, but he declined this dubious honor. Instead, he sent Hermes to ask Paris to make the choice. Paris was regarded as the most handsome of men then living so it seemed natural that he should make the decision.

To win Paris over, each of the goddesses offered to bribe Paris with something of value. Hera offered to make him the most powerful of men, a great king of the earth. Athena offered to make him the wisest, a man whose knowledge drew all from far and wide. But Aphrodite offered to give him the most beautiful woman in the world, Helen, wife of King Menelaus of Sparta. Paris did not hesitate in awarding the apple to Aphrodite. Hera and Athena (or Artemis) from then on became the implacable enemies of Paris, doing all they could to help his enemies among the Greeks. Paris spirited Helen away in his ship to Troy, causing the Greek leaders to convene a meeting and decide what to do.

Iphigenia in Aulis

The Greek leaders convened to plan a course of action. The leader of the Greeks was Agamemnon who was chosen because he ruled the mightiest Greek city and because he was also the brother of the offended party, King Menelaus of Sparta. The Goddess Artemis was angered because Agamemnon had offended her and she demanded the life of his daughter Iphigenia in sacrifice. Others say that the princess Iphigenia was sacrificed in order to give the Greeks a safe passage in their travels to Troy. Queen Clytemnestra, the wife of Agamemnon, pleaded with her husband not to sacrifice their daughter, but he ignored her. Therefore, Iphigenia was sacrificed at the altar in Aulis, earning Agamemnon the lifelong hatred of his wife Clytemnestra, a hatred that would destroy them all. This story would be the subject of dramas by Euripides and Sophocles, which served to render this myth one of the more well-known in the Greek canon.

Achilles and Patroclus

Achilles was the greatest hero on the Greek side during the Trojan War. he was the son of Peleus and Thetis, a nymph who was married to her husband in a lavish ceremony. Thetis feared for the safety of her son she dipped him as a babe in the waters of the River Styx, but she had to hold him by the ankle which left this spot vulnerable.

Achilles went to war on the Greek side joined by his dearest friend and companion Patroclus. There were many on the Trojan side who wanted to slay Achilles because of his prowess, but all attempts failed. Achilles also had enemies on the Greek side, especially Agamemnon with whom Achilles quarreled over the beautiful Briseis. This resulted in Achilles withdrawing from the war.

Patroclus later joined the war effort in Achilles stead. Patroclus was dressed in the famous armor of the Greek warrior. Achilles' friend was sought out by Hector, crown prince of Troy, and he was slain. I
n revenge, Achilles fought against Hector and this latter hero, too, was slain.

Achilles drew Hector's body around the walls of the city of Troy in his chariot until he finally agreed to give the body to Priam, the king of Troy and Hector's father.

The Death of Achilles

Revenge was sought by the Trojans for the way that their hero Hector had been treated by Achilles, even though the latter did eventually allow the Trojan prince to have an honorable burial. Paris would be the one to bring Achilles to his end. Some authors stated that it was Apollo who guided Paris's arrow on that fateful day. Whatever the case may be, Paris of Troy unleashed an arrow that hit the hero in his one weak spot, the ankle where his mother had held him when she dipped him into the River Styx.

The Aftermath: Agamemnon and Clytemnestra

The war would drag on until the Greeks had the idea of entering through the high walls of Troy by deception. They fashioned a giant wooden horse in which warriors could hide (on the inside), the famed Trojan Horse. The naive Trojans brought the Greek gift into their city, and during the night the warriors came in. They raised the gates and the inhabitants of Troy were slaughtered. The war was finally over. Agamemnon seemed lucky to get home in one piece, unlike Odysseus who would be left to journey the world for another ten years.

But Agamemnon would not be so lucky. His wife Clytemnestra still despised him for the sacrifice of their daughter Iphigenia all those years before. To add insult to injury, Agamemnon brought with him Cassandra, the famed princess of Troy whose prophecies, both Agamemnon and Cassandra would be murdered by Clytemnestra and her lover, Aegisthus. Agamemnon was drowned in a bathtub, while Clytemnestra would meet her own end at the hand of her vengeful children Electra and Orestes.

Chapter 11: Twenty Essential Facts about Greek Myth and Legend

Fact One: Hades was not counted among the Olympians.

There was some debate about which gods should be counted among the Olympians, but Hades certainly was not one of them. This is because Hades was the god of the underworld where he had his throne. Poseidon was also the ruler of a realm that was a division of the world, but because his throne was on Olympus he was counted as an Olympian. Hades's throne was not on Olympus so he was not counted among their number.

Fact Two: The oldest texts that detail the Ancient Greek gods are the Iliad and the Odyssey.

Greek myth is fortunate in that it has two canonical documents which can be used as sources for the essentials of Greek religion. The major gods and other creatures are all dealt with in these works, attesting to the fact that the basics of Greek religion were preserved relatively intact over a period of hundreds of years. It is believed that Homer lived in the 8th or 9th century BC, so that would place him about four hundred years before the golden age of Greek civilization.

Fact Three: Hades was not only the name of the god of the underworld but also of the underworld itself.

An interesting fact about Hades, the god of the underworld, is that his name was not only used for the god himself, but it also referred to the land which he ruled. So one can speak of so and so being sent to Hades (the place) and so forth.

Fact Four: Before the Olympian gods, there were the Titans.

Many fans of Greek mythology are aware of the Titans. Although not as famous as the Olympians, the Titans were the gods who preceded them.

Sometimes presented as giants, the Titans were not only the predecessors but also the ancestors of the Titans.

So Zeus and many other of the Olympian gods were actually the children of Cronus, who reigned as king of the Titans (and the universe) before he was overthrown by Zeus.

Fact Five: The Olympian gods overthrew the Titans to become rulers of the universe.

The Titans ruled before the Olympians. The Titans were often depicted as giants, and the war between the Olympians and Titans was sometimes called the Titanomachy or Gigantomachy (war of the giants). Cronus had been told a prophecy that he would be overthrown by his children so he swallowed them all. The last of them all was Zeus, but Cronus's wife Rhea gave her husband a stone swaddled in blankets instead of the babe. Zeus would grow up to slay his father and imprison the giants.

Fact Six: Zeus and his brothers drew lots to see who would control which of the three realms of the universe.

Zeus, Poseidon, and Hades drew lots to determine who would rule the sky, the sea, and the underworld. Although Zeus was the youngest, he drew the lot which allowed him to be king of the sky and overall king of the gods.

Poseidon drew the lot for the sea while Hades drew the lot for the underworld.

Fact Seven: Hera was not the first wife of Zeus.

Hera was the most famous, and certainly the most jealous, wife of Zeus. But she was not the first. Before Hera, there had been Metis. Metis would be the mother of Athena. Scholars debate whether Metis was actually a wife, but many claim her to be so. Zeus feared that his child with Metis would be more powerful and wiser than he so he swallowed her, but Athena would one day burst out of his skull with the help of Hephaestus (or some say Apollo or Hades).

Fact Eight: The exhaustive list of the Olympians is up for debate as some count Hestia among the number while others count Dionysus.

There were usually counted twelve gods among the Olympians, of which Zeus, Hera, Aphrodite, Apollo, Hermes, Ares, Hephaestus, Athena, Artemis, Poseidon, and Demeter were always counted. But the list compilers disagree on whether Dionysus or Hestia should be counted. Many lists count Dionysus as he is more famous in modern times, while others count Hestia as they argue that she was the oldest of all the Olympian gods and her worship was overall more significant than Dionysus's was.

Fact Nine: The Romans drew most of their gods from the pantheon of Greek gods and goddesses.

Even a cursory glance at the list of Roman deities reveals that the Romans received their gods from the Greeks. The Romans also saw their gods as residing on Mount Olympus and they counted the same gods as the Greeks did, only they gave them different names. The gods of the Romans were named Jupiter, Juno, Venus, Apollo, Mercury, Mars, Vulcan, Minerva, Diana, Neptune, and Ceres.

Fact Ten: Most Greek cities had their main temple devoted to their patron god, but there would have been other temples devoted to the rest of the divinities, too.

The Greek world is littered with ancient temples, of which the most famous are at places like Athens and Corinth, as well as in sites in Southern Italy and Sicily. It was common in the Greek world for there to be one large temple in each city or large town devoted to the patron god of the city. The main temple of Athens was thus the Parthenon, which was dedicated to Athena.

Fact Eleven: Zeus won a bet when Tiresias deemed that he was right about sex and not Hera. (The goddess struck him blind as a punishment).

Zeus and Hera had an interesting argument. The argument was about whether men or women derived more pleasure from sexual intercourse. Hera claimed that men derived more pleasure, while Zeus claimed that it was women who got the most out of the deed. A man called Tiresias, who had lived as both a man and a woman, determined that it was indeed the woman who derived the most pleasure, and in return, Hera struck him blind.

Fact Twelve: Hestia was the first of the Olympian gods to be born.

Hestia, sister of Zeus, was actually the first deity to be born to Cronus and Rhea, of the race of Titans. Cronus swallowed all of his children because he did not want his offspring to surpass him and overthrow him. Hestia was therefore not only the first child born but the first to be swallowed!

Fact Thirteen: Today, Cupid or Eros is often depicted as an infant, but he was originally described as a handsome youth.

Today, Cupid or Eros is usually depicted as a winged baby

shooting his arrows haphazardly at this or that, but in Ancient Greek times, he was actually a handsome youth.

This was the youth that had fallen in love with Psyche and was loved by her in return.

Fact Fourteen: Both Apollo and Helios were technically gods of the sun.

The Ancient Greeks actually had two gods of the sun. Apollo was a god of the sun (as well as a god of other things). and Helios was also a god of the sun. Some think of Helios as being the embodiment of the sun itself while Apollo was the god who controlled the sun and was responsible for the benefits of it. This state of affairs was later resolved by Helios becoming associated with Apollo as a version or identity of him, like an avatar.

Fact Fifteen: Both Artemis and Selene were goddesses of the moon.

This same situation also applied to the moon. Artemis was the goddess of the moon, but so was Selene. In much the same way that Apollo might be responsible for the sun while Helios was the sun itself, so too might Selene might be said to be the embodiment of the moon. In later times, Selene came to be adopted as an incarnation of Artemis (just like Apollo and Helios).

Fact Sixteen: Zeus was known to take on disguises when courting his love interests.

Zeus was famous not only for getting up to all sorts of mischief with the ladies but also for being a master of disguise when it came to this pursuit. The king of the gods courted Leda in the form of a swan, and he made love to Danae by coming to her in the form of golden rain.

Fact Seventeen: The Oracle at Delphi would give her prophecies in the form of cryptic answers to questions.

The Oracle of Delphi was said to speak the words that came to her from the god Apollo. But she did not speak these words in ordinary speech. Her answers were nearly always cryptic and had to be interpreted by her listeners in order to derive the true meaning. This oracle was consulted by Greeks from time immemorial, and it was said that this sibyl was originally devoted not to Apollo, but to Gaia, the earth goddess.

Fact Eighteen: One might say that it was Eris who was responsible for the Trojan War, not Paris.

Eris was the goddess of discord. She was a lesser-known goddess, but she made up for this state of affairs by triggering the Trojan War.

When she was not invited to the wedding of Peleus and Thetis, Eris got her revenge by dropping a golden apple into the throng. Upon the apple was written the words: "to the fairest." This act eventually led to Aphrodite promising Paris Helen as a reward for choosing her to be the prettiest. Therefore it would seem that Eris was to blame for this conflict and not Paris or Aphrodite (or even Helen herself).

Fact Nineteen: Greek mythology was practiced in regions outside the borders of modern-day Greece.

One of the most amazing facts about Greek mythology was that it was practiced outside of Greece. This was the religion of the Greeks wherever they lived, be it in Southern Italy, Sicily, Northern Africa, or the coasts of modern-day Turkey. Indeed, many of the great cities of "Greece" lay outside the traditional Greek homeland that we think of today.

Fact Twenty: Much of our information on Greek mythology comes not from the Greeks, but the Romans.

The Romans left us some very important works that helped to pass on the knowledge that originated with the Greeks. One of the most important of these was also among the more interesting. This was the Metamorphosis of Ovid. Among the tales told here were those of Cupid and Psyche and Athena and Arachne.

List of Greek Gods and Other Characters

Achelous: a river god who fought against Heracles for the hand of Deianira.

Achilles: Greek hero of the Trojan War. He belonged to the race of the Myrmidons. His beloved was Patroclus.

Adonis: the embodiment of male beauty and the beloved of Aphrodite.

Aegeus: King of Athens and father of Theseus.

Aeneas: prince of Troy and father to Romulus and Remus.

Agamemnon: King of Mycenae and husband of Clytemnestra.

Amazons: warrior women who often fought against the Greeks, as in the Trojan War.

Andromache: wife of Hector, son, and heir of King Priam of Troy.

Andromeda: daughter of the King of Ethiopia and wife to Perseus.

Antigone: faithful daughter of the unfortunate Oedipus.

Aphrodite: goddess of love; most likely originated outside of Greece.

Apollo: god of the sun, moderation, and all things masculine.

Arachne: a woman who challenged Athena to a competition and was transformed into a spider.

Ares: the Greek god of war.

Ariadne: princess of Crete who fell in love with Theseus and helped him find his way out of the Labyrinth. He later abandoned her on the island of Naxos.

Artemis: goddess of the hunt and the moon. Daughter to Leto and sister of Apollo.

Asclepius (Asclepius): son of Apollo and Greek god of medicine and health.

Astreus: A Titan who sired Boreas on Eos, the goddess of the dawn.

Athena: Greek goddess of wisdom and patroness of the city of Athens: daughter of Zeus and Metis.

Atlas: A Titan who was cursed to carry the sky on his shoulders for leading the Titans against the gods.

Atreus: ancestor of the House of Atreus, or Atreides, a family which included Agamemnon and Menelaus

Boreas: The North Wind. Boreas was the son of Eos, the dawn, and Astreus, a Titan.

Cassandra: daughter of Priam and famous because no one believed her prophecies. Apollo punished her with this ability after she was unfaithful.

Cassiopeia: wife of the King of Ethiopia and mother to Andromeda, the wife of Perseus. She became a constellation in the Northern Hemisphere along with her husband, Cepheus.

Castor and Pollux: sons of Leda. Castor was fathered by Tyndareus while Pollux (or Polydeuces) was fathered by Zeus.

Centaurs: infamous animals that were half man and half horse. Chiron was a gentle centaur who was the most famous of the lot.

Cepheus: the king of Ethiopia and father to Andromeda

Cerberus: the hound of the underworld.

Chiron: the most well-known of all of the centaurs.

Cronus: A Titan and the father of Zeus by his wife Rhea. He swallowed all of his children to prevent them from rising up against him.

Cybele: an important earth goddess associated with very ancient rites.

Daedalus: blacksmith of the gods.

Dardanus: according to Homer, this was the founder of the city of Troy, which featured at the center of the conflict of the Trojan War.

Dike: in Greek myth, Dike was the living personification of justice.

Dionysus: son of Zeus and god of wine. He was famous for the rituals surrounding his worship, which was known to the Romans as the Bacchanalia.

Echidna: a monstrous son of Gaia who was half man and half serpent.

Echo: a mountain nymph cursed by Hera to repeat her words again and again.

Eirene: the Greek personification of peace.

Endymion: a son of Zeus who fell in love with Selene, goddess of the moon.

Eos: goddess of the dawn.

Erebus: the personification of the darkness; father to Ether or Aether

Erechtheus: a king of Athens who was said to have the shape of a serpent

Erinyes: goddesses responsible for avenging a wrong.

Eris: the goddess of discord.

Eros (or Cupid): son of Aphrodite and a god of Love. He was known for his love of Psyche.

Gaia: the earth mother, she was the grandmother of Zeus. She was the mother of Uranus, Cronus, and several others.

Ganymede: a beautiful prince of Troy who was loved by Zeus. He was brought to Mount Olympus to serve the gods.

Hades: god of the underworld.

Hebe: daughter of Zeus and Hera, she served as cupbearer to the gods of Mount Olympus. It was said that she became the wife of Heracles after he was deified and brought to Olympus to live.

Hecate: an old goddess of the underworld.

Helen: daughter of Leda and Zeus and the wife of King Menelaus of Sparta. Her kidnapping by Paris triggered the Trojan War.

Helios: god of the sun, later identified with Apollo. His sacred place was Rhodes.

Hephaestus: the blacksmith of the gods.
Hera: wife of Zeus and queen of Olympus. She was also associated with childrearing and matronly affairs.
Heracles: a Greek hero famous for his twelve labors.
Hermes: messenger of the gods and son of Zeus.
Hestia: Goddess of the hearth.
Hyacinthus: a beautiful youth who was loved by Apollo. He was turned into a flower, the hyacinth.
Hygeia: the goddess of health.
Hypnos: the god of sleep.
Jason: a hero of Thessaly famous for leading the ship Argo and obtaining the Golden Fleece. He deserted his wife Medea for Glauca, princess of Corinth.
Icarus: a boy who flew too close to the sun with his wings.
Iphigenia: princess of Mycenae sacrificed by her father Agamemnon.
Laocoon: a Trojan priest who was punished for breaking his vow to the god Apollo.
Leda: a woman that Zeus courted in the form of a swan. She would give birth to Helen and Polydeuces by Zeus, and Castor and Clytemnestra by her husband Tyndareus.
Leto: the mother of Apollo and Artemis.
Medea: daughter of the king of Colchis and wife of Jason. Later the wife of King Aegeus of Athens.
Menelaus: the king of Lacedaemon (Sparta) and husband of Helen in the Iliad.

Metis: first wife of Zeus and mother to Athena.

Minos: the king of Crete and father to Ariadne.

Minotaur: the half man and half bull of the Labyrinth. He was a possession of King Minos.

Narcissus: a beautiful youth who was enamored of his own reflection. He was transformed into a flower.

Oceanus: Titan who was the god of the oceans.

Oedipus: a Greek who was the unfortunate target of a prophecy that he would kill his father and marry his mother, which he eventually did.

Pegasus: a winged horse that was created from the blood of Medusa's head. He became the possession of Perseus.

Perseus: one of the most famous of Greek heroes, Perseus was the son of Princess Danae of Argos who was imprisoned by her father in an attempt to circumvent a prophecy. He would slay the Medusa, rescue Princess Andromeda, and eventually fulfill the oracle's prophecy of slaying his grandfather.

Persephone: wife of Hades and resident of the underworld.

Phaeton: a son of Helios who asked his father to drive his chariot. He was unable to control the chariot and wound up scorching the earth.

Poseidon: god of the sea.

Prometheus: a Tritan who was punished for giving fire to Man by being chained to a rock and picked at by birds.

Rhea: wife of Cronos and mother of Zeus, Hera, and most of the other Olympian gods and goddesses.

Selene: goddess and embodiment of the moon. Later identified with Artemis.

Sphinx: a creature with wings that was part human and part animal.

Theseus: one of the most famous Greek heroes. He slew the Minotaur and became king of Athens.

Thetis: the mother of Achilles who dipped him into the waters of the Styx for protection.

Uranus: A Titan and grandfather to Zeus.

Zeus: the king of the gods and god of the sky. The leader of the Olympian pantheon.

Frequently Asked Questions

1. Was Greek mythology and legend confined to modern-day Greece?

Greek myth and legend applied to the Greek world, which extended beyond the bounds of modern-day Greece. Indeed, until the 20th century, Greek-speaking people also lived on the Western coast of what is now Turkey, where they had been living since at least 1000 BC, so about 3000 years. As a result of the war between Greece and Turkey, most of these people had to move to the modern-day nation of Greece.

But even leaving aside the Greek coast of Turkey, Greeks had settled throughout the Mediterranean region. They had even settled as far as the Black Sea where they had planted many colonies, most of which were founded by the Ionian city of Miletus. But the most prosperous cities of the Greek diaspora were in Southern Italy and on the island of Sicily. Here, the Greeks found a fertile and thinly-populated land. They were able to plant colonies and grow grain that was exported to the rest of the Greek world well into the Roman period. The people who settled here were Greeks and they carried Greek traditions with them in their new homes.

2. What was the period of time associated with the practice of Greek religion?

Greek history was divided into several periods. The earliest period is usually called the Mycenean period, and it was an early golden age associated with art and architectural sites, including Ancient Mycenae, near Argos. This was followed by a Dark Age, during which Greece was overrun by various tribes of invaders. Although it seems unusual, all the groups that lived in Greece were regarded as Greeks, or Hellenes, even though they may have come from different places and had settled in Greece in different times.

The Dark Ages was followed by the Archaic Period, during which time the Greeks began to experience cultural growth and artistic prominence again. This period was also associated with colonization of other regions and the beginning of democratic and oligarchic institutions as most Greek kings were overthrown or otherwise disappeared. Then there was the Classical Age, which was the golden age of Greek mythology, art, and culture. Finally, there was the Hellenistic Age, which resulted when Alexander carried Greek culture (and Greek people) to new lands to the East. This last period was also associated with the rise of Rome.

3. Should Greek gods and goddesses and the associated belief system be termed a religion or was it something else?

It may seem strange to term a mythological system of belief a religion because of our modern idea of what religion entails, but this is precisely what this belief system was. Religion involves a spiritual belief about a deity or deities and it comes with a system of worship that is usually ritualized. Although the ancient Greek gods and goddesses had lives that took the form of what we might call a soap opera today, the Greek people of ancient times believed in this cast of characters, and the worship of them was a fundamental part of their lives.

Modern scholars often refer to the myths and legends of the Ancient Greeks as the Ancient Greek religion. Many modern religions are monotheistic so common people often associate pagan ways of life as something other than a religion like a folk belief or shamanism. There certainly were earthy elements in the Greek religion, although they had been overplayed by the supposedly more recent patriarchal elements that were said to come from the invaders from the north during the Dark Ages. Whatever your personal opinion is on the relative merits of ancient Greek belief, it certainly meets the standard of religion.

4. What is an epithet, and what is the significance of epithets in Ancient Greek religion?

An epithet is a description that is part of a name; it sometimes follows a name though it may come before. Examples include swift-footed Achilles, the rosy-cheeked Dawn, and Aphrodite, the foam-born. An epithet is essentially an attribute of that person, whether god, hero, or another mortal, but it has a special meaning because the particular attribute is well-known enough to be closely associated with that person.

Epithets were important because they were often associated with the gods, and in this role, they represented a realm of power and consequently of devotion for the gods. In other words, there were many epithets of Zeus that represented different domains of this god. Zeus, therefore, may have different roles in different places where he was revered. This was especially true of deities of foreign origin, or deities that assumed the identities of other regional deities. Apollo and Aphrodite had many epithets associated with their role in the particular region or city where they were worshipped.

5. Were all the gods of Ancient Greece Olympians?

All of the main gods of Ancient Greece were Olympians, although we have been introduced to many other gods that were not.

For example, the Titans who preceded the Olympians were not classed as Olympians. Also, there were a number of gods, especially those that were the personifications of things, that were not classed as Olympians. So Eos, goddess of the dawn, and Boreas, the North Wind, would not have been considered Olympians, generally. Also, Hypnos, the god of sleep, or Hygeia, goddess of health, also would not have been considered Olympians. It is even worth debating whether Asclepius, god of medicine, was an Olympian.

6. Who were the nymphs and why do they appear so frequently in Greek legend?

Nymphs are essentially the embodied spirits of physical spaces, even if those spaces were changing (like water). They occupied a liminal space between god and mortal. Although they are not properly termed demigods, they had much in common with this particular group. Demigods were essentially the half-mortal children of the gods, and they typically had longer life spans and special accouterments that distinguished them from human beings. Although the same is not true of the naiads, nereids, and others, it is true that these creatures or spirits were believed to basically be immortal when it came to the duration of life, although they could be killed as mortals can.

Nymph is basically the catch-all term for the spirit characters discussed in this portion of the chapter. Nereids and naiads are types of nymphs. Nymphs were generally depicted (and thought of) as beautiful young girls. They were associated with fertility and fecundity. Many gods and demigods were the children on nymphs, including characters like Achilles. A nymph was the beautiful young girl associated with (usually) a body of water. A nereid was a nymph associated with the sea, while a naiad was usually associated with a discrete aqueous structure, like a fountain. Although there were no cities or temples associated with nymphs, they frequently appeared in myth and legend. Shrines devoted to important local nymphs would have been common in the Greek world.

7. Was there an element of historicity in Greek myth or was it all made up?
This is an interesting and important question. Although it may seem at first glance that all of Greek myth and legend was invented, scholars believe that certain characters, even godly ones, might have been real. For example, historians believe that Theseus and Heracles were probably real characters. Theseus was the mythological king of Athens who defeated the Minotaur, while Heracles was the son of Zeus who overcame twelve labors and eventually was made a god.

Of course, the picture becomes murkier when we examine other characters. This is because it is nearly impossible to prove (or disprove) that a particular character, even a human one, was real or fantasy. The same can be said of Norse mythology. It is not always clear here whether characters were real or fantasy, especially as many of the sagas included people that actually lived, such as attested kings of Denmark and Norway. Because the Ancient Greeks lived so long ago, it is hard to find evidence that this person lived or did not. Suffice it to say, it is safe to assume that some ancient kings and heroes of myth, such as Menelaus and Agamemnon of the Trojan War, might have lived, while others like Achilles or Hector might have been created by storytellers.

8. What about the Trojan War? Was that an actual historic event?

This is a perfect caveat to a discussion about the Trojan War. As we have examined so far, it is difficult to tell who in myth lived or did not, especially when it comes to human characters where we know that they actually might have lived. The Trojan War period is a popular time to discuss when it comes to historicity because archaeologists have discovered finds from Mycenae and Troy from about the same time. Archaeologists have even labeled certain finds as belonging to Agamemnon or Priam based on their assumptions about the real identity of buried kings, their treasures, and so on.

If we leave aside the characters and talk about the Trojan War as an event, historians do believe that a war was fought at the site of Troy, or Ilium. Archaeologists have found more than ten different historical cities at the site of Troy; meaning that cities were successively destroyed and abandoned and subsequently built over. There is a large city at the site from the 12th century BC, about the same time as another major city at Mycenae, that appears to have been destroyed in that century, which led the archaeologist Heinrich Schliemann to believe that he had not only found Troy but that he had proved that the Trojan War actually occurred.

9. Is it true that some of the Greek gods originated outside of Greece?

The origin of this god or that is an interesting subject to explore because it allows one to get a real sense of cultural exchange as it occurs over time. Only the most isolated societies do not adopt some features of the religions of their neighbors. A major exception, of course, is the Egyptians who were so far ahead of anyone around them that they had no peers from whom to borrow deities or religious practices.

But the Greeks certainly adopted gods from other peoples during their history.

First of all, it is believed that the original inhabitants of Greece worshipped gods who were primarily female. These were allegedly deities associated with fertility, the home, and peace. Several waves of invaders brought other gods - so-called sky gods like Zeus. Even later, exposure to foreign peoples brought to the Greeks gods like Aphrodite, Dionysus, and others. It has even suggested that some gods of Ancient Greece may have originally been female and were changed later into male deities.

10. Why is it important to understand the history of Ancient Greece when discussing mythology?
Learning about the history of Ancient Greece when studying mythology allows you to develop a context for the story that mythology entails. Mythologies provide valuable information about the characteristics of a people, and examining history as well allows one to complete the picture. For example, the existence of male and female gods in Olympus with slightly different roles does seem to support the idea that waves of invasions changed the character of the Ancient Greek religion from having matriarchal elements to being overwhelmingly patriarchal. So the conflict between Zeus and Hera can actually be interpreted as representing a tension between a new patriarchal system and an older matriarchal one.

11. Who were the Dorians and why were they important to the Greek story?

The Dorians were invaders who came from the North during the period in Greek history known as the Dark Ages. They were one of the three major groups of Greeks during the Classical period along with the Ionians and the Aeolians. These groups spoke different dialects of Greek and had cultural practices that were specific to them. The legacy of Dorian invasion was apparent in later Greece, especially in Sparta where the Dorian invaders ruled over the conquered natives. Indeed, the successive invasions from the north may have contributed to the relative backwardness of decline associated with the Dark Ages period.

12. Where did the Greeks come from?

Evidence suggests that the Ancient Greeks were descended from several peoples who lived in the area of modern-day Greece at different times. The earliest inhabitants of Greece may have been similar to the early inhabitants of other areas of the Northern Mediterranean Sea, such as Italy and Turkey. These people are sometimes referred to as Pelasgians, and they may be the same as the so-called Sea Peoples who are attested in other sources. These people would have been assimilated or conquered by successive waves of people.

It is not clear when the first wave of conquerors came, but they likely came sometime before the Mycenaean and Trojan War period, so the 13th - 12th centuries BC. Afterward, Greece fell into a Dark Age where there were more invasions. It seems that the conquerors adopted the Greek spoken language because there is no evidence for major language differences across Ancient Greece. That being said, there was evidence for dialects or regional languages (much like the regional languages of Spain and Italy), which suggests waves of people coming from different places or, at the very least, divergence over time. In short, the Greeks were at least partially descended from very early native inhabitants of the peninsula followed by others who came later and generally assimilated with the original inhabitants. There is evidence for this picture in the puzzle piece picture of gods (patriarchal and matriarchal) in Greek myth and legend.

13. Was Athena an important goddess in the Greek world, or was she only important because of her association with the city of Athens?

One of the amazing things about Greek gods and goddesses is that they had regional affiliations. Certain gods and goddesses had cities that were sacred to them and which they served as the protectors of.

Athena was the patron goddess of Athens, a city which had been named after her. This patron status meant that the main temple of the city was devoted to that god or goddess, and it would have been in a prominent place in town, usually the acropolis.

In the case of Athena, she does seem to be an important goddess in the Greek world, but her status was certainly improved by the prominence of Athens. Athens's place as the largest and most important Greek city meant that they could embellish Athena's temple, the Parthenon until it became one of the largest in the Greek world. The cult of Athena would also be spread by means of propaganda in the form of statues and other artistic wares. Even drama was a way to promote the status of one god vis a vis another.

14. Is Zeus basically the equivalent of Odin in Norse myth?

Patriarchal societies generally have a sky god who is often also the king of the gods. This was true of the Ancient Greeks as well as the Norse. So, in short, yes, Odin is basically the Norse equivalent of Zeus.

Odin was called All-Father in Norse tradition, and he basically modeled the role that the ideal male was meant to play in his community.

Therefore, it was important in patriarchal societies for the gods and their relationship with one another to serve as a model for how relationships should be in society. Just like Odin, Zeus was the king of his castle, although Zeus's castle was called Mount Olympus while Odin's was known as Asgard.

15. Why is Greek mythology less popular in modern media than Norse characters like Thor?

Well, it is not necessarily true that Greek mythological characters are less popular or less influential than Norse ones. Norse mythology has been promoted recently because a particular character (Thor) has been associated with a well-liked and very popular franchise. That being said, Ancient Greek characters also have a prominent place both in media and literature. In particular, Heracles (or Hercules as he was known in Rome) has been a popular character in film since films became popular. Movies about this character have been made right up through to the present.

Even relatively recent films like *Clash of the Titans* are based on the Greek myth. This film is essentially the story of Perseus's battle against the gorgon Medusa and other, which were important stories in Ancient Greece.

These stories are often highly dramatized but still reflect both the role of gods in the society and also the role of the hero.

As modern society is constructed differently, both the religious element and the hero element have lost their essential meaning and basically become relegated to the realm of fantasy.

16. What impact has the Ancient Greek religion had on life and society today?

The Ancient Greeks were the first to produce drama as we know it. The dramas of the Greeks displayed the characters of Greek myth and their interaction with the gods. The common thread in Greek drama was often hubris, that is, pride against the gods. An oracle would proclaim a future ordained by the gods and the proud mortal would do everything they could to circumvent it. In the end, their attempts to prevent the future the oracle declared served only to create it. This is seen not only in Oedipus but in other Greek dramas.

Another area of Greek influence today is in the realm of philosophy. Greek philosophers laid the groundwork for the philosophy of today. They developed the method of instructing students and even established the first schools of philosophy. Although Ancient Greek philosophy was not as closely tied to myth and legend as the drama was, it was the world of myth and superstition that created the first philosophers and poets: men who wanted to break away from a world that they saw as mired in ignorance and backwardness.

17. Is Greek mythology the same as Roman mythology?

Most of the gods and other characters of Roman mythology come from the Greeks. The Romans would have been exposed to Greek myths and other aspects of Greek culture from about the 6th or 7th century BC onward. It was at this time that the Greeks began establishing colonies in Southern Italy and Sicily. Greece had an enormous impact on the Romans, and religion is only the most obvious example. That being said, the Romans did not get all of their religion from the Greeks.

Indeed, we can talk about Roman religion in much the same way that we can talk about Greek religion. Roman religion was not peripheral to Roman life just as Greek religion was not peripheral to Greek life. Importantly, the Romans worshipped gods that they did not derive from the Greeks. Whether these gods were derived from the Etruscans or they were native to the Romans themselves is a question that is still up for debate. Some of the Roman gods were clearly of a very ancient origin. They were often grouped together in large groups, and they might be faceless or lacking a distinct identity as individuals. Examples of grouped Roman gods include the Lares. The Romans also engaged in a form of ancestor worship.

18. How did Greek myth and legend spread to Rome?

Greek myth and legend spread to Rome through contact

between the Greeks and Romans. This contact occurred due to the close proximity of Greek colonies to the burgeoning Rome. Some of these cities are still existing today, such as Naples and Taranto in Southern Italy, and Syracuse on Sicily. Roman merchants and other travelers would have been exposed to not only Greek myths about gods and heroes, but Greek dramas, Greek art, and Greek historic tradition. Although these latter two categories were not explicitly mythological, they would have helped to reinforce the myths and legends that the Romans had already begun to receive from the Greeks.

19. Where are the best-preserved Greek temples located?

There are many examples of temples in modern-day Greece. For example, the Parthenon, Theseum, Erechtheum, and other temples in Athens have been preserved and are frequently visited by tourists. There are also other sites like Corinth and Rhodes were temple complexes remain to this day. With that said, some of the greatest examples of Greek temples and other Greek architecture actually exists outside of modern-day Greece. There are numerous sites in Turkey, such as Ephesus, Halicarnassus, Priene, and others, where Greco-Roman remains, are visible. Arguably the best-preserved temple sites are located in Italy, where numerous temples can be found.

20. Are the depictions of Greek gods in movies like Clash of the Titans and the Immortals accurate or is it all just invented for dramatic effect?

It is difficult for us today to really know how the Greeks perceived their gods though we can guess. Greek drama, art, and other media give us an idea of how the Greeks perceived their gods both physically and intellectually. The Greeks seemed to view their gods as being quarrelsome like people and sometimes fickle, but because they were powerful and, frankly, gods, they had to be obeyed or those who did not risk suffering the consequences. In movies like *Clash of the Titans* Greek gods are portrayed much like they are in art. They also have the fickleness and obsession with humans that works of drama and literature seem to suggest. So, in short, the movies seem to do a pretty good job at displaying the gods as the Greeks would have seen them, even if the meaning these gods would have to people today is very different.

21. Who was the most important god in the Greek pantheon?

There is a strong regional component to much of the worship of the Gods in the Greek world. So Athena was important in certain places and Artemis was important in others.
But major gods and goddesses would see their worship widespread in the Greek world. For example, because most

Greeks lived near the sea (including many people who lived on islands), Poseidon was worshipped practically everywhere. This was also true of gods like Dionysus and Hermes. But arguably the two most important gods were Zeus and Apollo.

Although Apollo embodied masculinity, we would have to say that Zeus, as king of the gods, was most important. His temple at Olympia, where the Olympic Games were held, was one of the largest on the Greek world. It had a large statue of gold and ivory, which depicted Zeus sitting on a throne. Indeed, the Olympic Games were staged in order to honor Zeus. Although there were other multi-city games held around the Greek world, like the Isthmic Games held at Isthmia near Corinth, the Olympian Games were the most important.

But back to Zeus... Zeus was the king of the gods and he was also associated with the sky. He had a role in weather, too, as the Greeks believed that thunderbolts were hurled to the earth by Zeus. Zeus was not only the king of the gods, but he was also the father of many of them. Zeus is featured in many myths of the Ancient Greeks, even if he is on the sidelines interfering in one way or the other. The role that Zeus plays echoes the role of a father-king in patriarchal societies, as Greece and Rome both were. In Rome, Zeus was known as Jupiter.

As powerful as Zeus was, he was not alone in heading his tribe of Olympians. He had to share his role with Hera, his wife. Hera, therefore, plays a more important role than the goddess wives in other mythologies, like Norse myth, for example. The role of Hera is something that Greek writers never allowed their readers to forget. Zeus presided over the Olympian gods side-by-side with Hera. In fact, Zeus often had to fix the problems that Hera created. Of course, most of these "problems" originate with Zeus's wandering eye, which served as a constant trigger for the ire of his wife, Hera.

22. Who were the Amazons?
The Amazons were famous female warriors who were said to live at the world's edge, which to some meant Asia Minor, while others placed them in Africa. The Amazons were under the special protection of Artemis, a goddess who regarded the hunt and all wild things as sacred.

As the Amazons were somewhat wild, at least in the uncivilized fashion in which they lived, it seems sensible that they would be under her protection. The Amazons were said to kidnap men and use them as studs to sire strong children. They only selected the best men for this task. Naturally, patriarchal Greek society viewed this practice (and the women who engaged in it) with horror. It has been argued by some that the Amazon myth may have originated with warlike Scythian warriors who lived on the Russian steppes.

They may have had warrior women in their ranks, providing ample imaginative fodder to Ancient Greek audiences who seemed inclined to believe everything.

There were many legends about the Amazons. Some writers asserted that the warrior women cut off one of their breasts to allow better use of their bow arm. Though this tale is commonly told, it has been portrayed in ancient art.

23. Who were the demigods?
Demigod was a catch-all term for the children of the gods who were not gods. Children of nymphs or other semi-divine creatures might also be considered demigods. Demigods were usually sired by a father who was a divinity and a mother who was a mortal, nymph, or other non-divine characters. Demigods were given a special name because they often had divine attributes associated with them, such as a fair and pleasing appearance, long life, better than normal strength, or some other skill that set them apart from the other run of the mill human beings that were encountered in Greek myth and legend.

Greek myth is unique in setting these particular characters apart as special. In many other mythologies, the children of gods by mortals are usually just human beings, though in some cases they might be adopted among the gods.

As the gods were practically a race apart from human beings it seems strange that they would take such a fancy to mortals as to reproduce with them. There were enough gods around that Zeus, Apollo, and others could have had their pick. Stranger still that the gods seemed not only inclined to procreate with mortals but that the offspring of these unions seemed to be special targets of their attention.

24. What were the names of the Argonauts?

The Argonauts were the warriors who ventured to the land of Colchis to find the Golden Fleece, the golden skin of a sheep. They sailed in the ship Argo and were led by Jason. According to scholar Robert Graves, the following is the list of men and women who went on the voyage.

Acastus

Actor, of Phocis

Admetus, of Pherae

Amphiaraus, of Argos

Ancaeus, of Samos

Argus, shipbuilder

Ascalphus, demigod, son of Ares

Asterius, of Pelopia

Atalanta, a huntress

Augeias, a native of Elis

Butes, a native of Athens

Caeneus, a Lapith

Calais, son of Boreas, the North Wind

Canthus, of Euboea

Castor, along with Pollux or Polydeuces, one of the Dioscuri

Cepheus, son of Aleus of Arcadia

Corionis, another Lapith

Echion, demigod, son of Hermes

Erginus, a native of Miletus

Euphemus

Euryalus

Heracles, demigod, son of Zeus

Hylas, friend, and companion to Heracles

Idas, of Messene

Idmon, demigod, son of Apollo and native of Argos

Iphicles

Iphitus, of Mycenae

Laertes, of Argos

Lynceus, a brother to Idas

Melampus, demigod, son of Poseidon

Meleager, a native of Calydon

Mopsus, yet another Lapith

Naupilus, demigod, son of Poseidon and native of Argos

Oileus, brother to Ajax, a well-known hero

Orpheus, a poet

Palaemon, demigod, son of Hephaestus

Peleus, a member of the race of Myrmidons

Peneleos, a native of Boetia

Periclymenus, demigod, son of Poseidon
Phalerus, a native of Athens
Phanus, demigod, a native of Crete and son to Dionysus
Poeas, a native of Magnesia
Polydeuces (or Pollux), brother to Castor and one of the Dioscuri
Polyphemus, a native of Arcadia
Staphylus, a native of Crete and brother to Phanus
Typhus, the ship's helmsman on the Argo
Zetes, another son of Boreas

25. Who were the love interests of Zeus?

Zeus, as king of the gods, had many love interests. These included his two wives, in addition to others. The love interests of Zeus included the following: Metis, first wife and mother of Athena; Hera, mother of Hephaestus, Ares, and Hebe; Electra; Eurynome; Io; Leda; Leto; Maia; Mnemosyne; Themis; Antiope; Danae; Niobe; Semele. There was also Demeter and Lamia, whose children were slain by Hera.

26. Who were the children of Zeus?

Zeus was the father of Athena, Hera, Hephaestus, and Hebe. By a certain Electra, Zeus was the father of Harmonia. Zeus fathered the Three Graces by Eurynome. Leto was the mother of Apollo and Artemis. Hermes was the son of Zeus by Maia.

Mnemosyne was the mother of the Muses, all daughters. Themis, the embodiment of the law, gave birth to several children including the Horae, Eunomia, Dike, the Fates, and Eirene, whose name means peace. Children of Zeus by mortal women include Amphion, Zethus, Perseus, Epaphus, Castor, Pollux (or Polydeuces), Argos (who founded the city of Argos), and Dionysius, who was the son of Semele.

27. What were the Twelve Labors of Heracles (Hercules)?

First Labor: The Nemean Lion

Second Labor: The Hydra of Lernea

Third Labor: The Wild Boar of Erymanthus

Fourth Labor: The Hind of Ceryneia

Fifth Labor: The Stymphalian Birds

Sixth Labor: The Augean Stables

Seventh Labor: The Cretan Bull

Eighth Labor: The Horses of Diomedes

Ninth Labor: The Girdle of the Amazon

Tenth Labor: Geryon's Cattle

Eleventh Labor: The Theft of Cerberus

Twelfth Labor: The Golden Apples of Hesperides

Conclusion

Greek myth and legend will continue to fascinate adults and children around the world for many years to come. It may seem strange to us but to the Ancient Greeks these tales of gods and heroes, of monsters and nymphs, of angry deities exacting revenge on proud mortals: these were not fantasying but events in real religion. The Ancient Greeks told and heard these stories as part of a ritual that taught them how to live. Greek myths taught the men and women of Ancient Greek how to interact with the gods and what to expect from life.

The Ancient Greek religion has been left to us today in nearly complete form. That is, we know a great deal more about the Ancient Greek religion than we do about say the religion of the Ancient Egyptians or the Etruscans. Indeed, the Ancient Greek religion and the enduring fascination with it is just one way in which people who lived more than two thousand years ago continue to influence us today. We see all around us Greek influence in art and architecture, but we also see Greek influence in our traditions of philosophy and drama. Though these may seem to be distinct realms that the Greeks have left to us, they truly represent different sides of the same coin.

You were introduced to the Greeks by first learning about the world in which they lived. The Greek world exists in a similar form today as it did thousands of years ago. The Greek peninsula is a rocky and mostly inhospitable land hugged by the sea. It consists of many islands whose coasts abound in fish and all the other products of the sea. The Greek people of the past were just as industrious then as they were today. They were also warlike, warring amongst each other so animatedly that they would fall easy prey to the rising power of Rome.

At the center of Ancient Greek myth and legend were the gods themselves. The chief gods of Ancient Greece were the Olympians, but there were many others, among whom we may count the spirits of the rivers, trees, and seas, who were known respectively as nymphs, dryads, and nereids. There were also the gods of the four winds, the Fates, the Muses, and many others. The primary gods were Zeus, Apollo, and Athena, but Hera, Dionysus, Aphrodite, Hermes, and others were both worshipped and feared all across the Greek world.

Just as in other mythologies, the gods fathered many children. And they did not discriminate, being just as fond of mortal women as they were of goddesses and nymphs. Many Greek myths center around the children of the gods, and some of the most famous heroes of Greek mythology were such children.

So no exploration of Greek mythology would be complete without detailing the lives of Heracles, Perseus, and Helen, all of whom were children of Zeus, the king of the gods.

These heroes were another important segment in Greek myth, right alongside the gods. Indeed, one might even argue that when it came to the essential symbolism of Greek myth and the purpose it served in the society the heroes were more important than the gods, even if they were dubious heroes like Oedipus. These characters instructed the Greeks of the time on what life was and how to deal with it. Greek civilization may have been very different if their imagination had not created such startling characters.

In the end, Greek mythology comes across as an elaborate drama, but it is more than that. The story of the Twelve Labors of Heracles was really a series of lessons on how to deal with the travails of life. The Trojan War was another lesson on the fundamental aspects of mankind. Men went to war over women. Men bickered with one another over various and sundry silly things. And men always had to answer for unjust deeds, just as Agamemnon had to answer for the sacrifice of Iphigenia.

www.ingramcontent.com/pod-product-compliance
Lightning Source LLC
Chambersburg PA
CBHW051705160426
43209CB00004B/1030